INVISIBLE LEASHES

Allison Christina Gainer

INVISIBLE LEASHES

Service Dogs, Institutional Barriers, and the Fight for Authentic Access in Higher Education

Disability Studies

Collection Editor
Damian Mellifont

LPP

First published in 2025 by Lived Places Publishing

British Library Cataloguing in Publication Data
A CIP record for this book is available from the British Library.

ISBN: 9781915271693 (pbk)
ISBN: 9781915271716 (ePDF)
ISBN: 9781915271709 (ePUB)

Cover design by Fiachra McCarthy
Book design by Rachel Trolove of Twin Trail Design
Typeset by Newgen Publishing, UK

Lived Places Publishing
P.O. Box 1845
47 Echo Avenue
Miller Place, NY 11764

www.livedplacespublishing.com

Abstract

Invisible leashes is the story of what it's really like to move through the halls of higher education as a disabled professional and doctoral student, never alone—always with Lily-Rue, a service dog who's as much companion as co-pilot. Part memoir, part policy critique, the book pulls back the curtain on the invisible barriers that linger even in schools and universities that swear they're inclusive.

Most people don't see the obstacles. They don't notice the way doors—literal and metaphorical—stay closed to anyone who doesn't fit the mold. For those of us with nonapparent or shifting disabilities, the hardest part is often having to prove, repeatedly, that we belong. Every meeting, every classroom, every "accommodation" request becomes a small battle: to be seen, to be understood, to be allowed to exist without apology or explanation.

Lily-Rue, my service dog, isn't just there to help with daily life. She's a walking reminder that some things need to be visible, even when society would rather, we keep them hidden. Together, we navigate not just the physical world but also the emotional and professional minefields that come with being "different" in spaces designed for sameness.

Through stories, snapshots, and sharp analysis, *Invisible leashes* calls out ableist systems and policies that still fall short—and argues that access shouldn't be a favor or an afterthought. It's an invitation for anyone who's ever felt like a disruption just for being themselves. More than anything, it's a plea to universities and other institutions: stop pretending at inclusion. Build something real, rooted in equity and the full, unapologetic presence and inclusion of disabled people.

Key words

Disability advocacy, disability rights, disability identity, invisible disabilities, chronic illness, neurodivergence, academic ableism, institutional barriers, policy reform, accessibility

Contents

Content warning

This book contains personal stories and reflections that may be difficult for some readers. Topics explored include ableism, disability discrimination, chronic illness, mental health challenges, medical gaslighting, institutional barriers, grief, anxiety, depression, and the emotional realities of living with a disability. There are also discussions of disability disclosure, service animal use, and navigating exclusion in educational and workplace settings.

Please know that these stories come from my own lived experiences as a disabled person and service dog handler. My perspective is uniquely my own and does not represent all disabled people. Disability experiences vary widely, and no two journeys are exactly the same. My hope in sharing these truths is not to speak for others, but to invite thoughtful reflection, encourage more compassionate practices, and push for meaningful change in systems that often overlook or exclude us.

Some sections may bring up strong emotions or uncomfortable memories, especially if you have faced similar challenges. I encourage you to care for yourself as you read. Take breaks if you need to, skip sections if necessary, and return only when you feel ready.

Your comfort and well-being matter. Please honor them throughout this reading experience.

Learning objectives

As you read this book, my hope is that you will:

1. Gain a clearer understanding of navigating higher education and professional spaces as informed by a disabled person.
2. Recognize how ableism and institutional barriers can quietly shape policies, relationships, and everyday experiences for disabled students and employees.
3. Explore the complicated, often personal journey of claiming disability identity, especially when living with dynamic or nonapparent disabilities.
4. Learn more about the unique role of service dogs in the lives of disabled people—including both the essential support they provide and the misconceptions that often surround them.
5. Reflect on the emotional weight that comes with disclosing a disability, asking for accommodations, or simply existing in spaces that weren't built with us in mind.
6. Understand why true accessibility means more than following policies—it means creating spaces where people are safe, included, and valued without having to fight for it.
7. Consider how you can show up as an ally, advocate, or supporter, whether in classrooms, workplaces, or your community.

8. Begin to see disability not just through the lens of compliance or accommodation, but as an important part of social justice and equity conversations.

Above all, this book invites you to listen, reflect, and imagine what could change if we all moved through the world with a little more care, curiosity, and commitment to inclusion.

Preface

But before we begin, there's something I need to get off my chest, something I wish I'd heard, really heard, from someone else when my own life started to unravel. Disability can be lonely.

Not the kind of loneliness you fix by texting a friend or filling the room with people. Not the kind a movie night or a crowded party can cure. This is a different breed entirely: the solitude that creeps in when your body rebels against you and the world pretends nothing's wrong. It's the silence between you and the rest of humanity, the ache that settles so deep you start to wonder if it's become part of your DNA.

You learn early: when your illness doesn't show on the surface, people don't see it, don't believe it, and if you're honest most of them just don't want to deal with it. They want the version of you that doesn't make things awkward, that doesn't need special treatment, who laughs off the hard parts and always "rallies" when plans are made. They want you to be easy. And so, you learn to be easy, or at least to fake it. You practice smiling through pain, nodding when people say, "But you look great!" as if that's a compliment and not a dismissal. You memorize all the ways to minimize your needs, to apologize for your existence, to shrink yourself to fit the space you're allowed.

The costs pile up, quietly at first. There are the obvious things: the appointments you must schedule and reschedule, the bills that show up in thick white envelopes, the medication bottles rattling in your bag. But those are just the beginning. The bigger losses are the invisible ones, the ones you feel but can't name right away. Like the job you didn't even apply for because you knew you couldn't hack the hours. The friend who stopped inviting you because you canceled one too many times. The lover who grew tired of adjusting. The feeling of missing out on your own life, of becoming a bystander to your own story.

It's a special kind of grief, waking up in a body that won't do what you ask and then spending the rest of the day trying to convince everyone else that you're not making it up. You become an actor in your own life, rehearsing lines for every scenario. You learn to anticipate the questions: "Are you sure you can't just push through?" "Have you tried yoga?" "Maybe if you got more sleep?" You get good at editing your story, leaving out the worst moments, sanding down the sharp edges so people won't flinch. You learn to say "I'm fine" when you're anything but, because the alternative is too complicated, too heavy, too risky.

There's a cost to this constant performance—a cost that's hard to tally, because it's paid out in quiet, daily installments. Every time you swallow the truth because you know it'll make someone uncomfortable, you lose a little piece of yourself. Every time you force your body to keep up, knowing you'll pay for it later, you chip away at your reserves. Every time you ask for help and see the flicker of annoyance in someone's eyes, you shrink a bit more, until smallness feels like safety.

The world is designed for people who move through it without having to explain themselves. Doors open, stairs are climbed, plans are made without a second thought. For the rest of us, every step is a negotiation. You scan every room for the nearest exit, you clock the distance to the bathroom, you weigh whether you have the energy to fake normalcy one more time. You become a master of logistics, a strategist, a reluctant expert in making it work. But sometimes you just want to let your guard down, to say, "This is really hard," without fearing you'll be accused of exaggerating or worse, seeking attention.

What no one tells you about having a dynamic, nonapparent disability is how much time you spend managing other people's discomfort. You become fluent in disclaimers, always ready to explain why you're limping today when you weren't yesterday, or why you need to rest when you looked fine an hour ago. You worry about being seen as unreliable, flaky, high maintenance. You worry about being pitied. You worry about being resented. You worry about being forgotten.

It's exhausting, living with this kind of vigilance. You start to second-guess your own reality. Was the pain really that bad, or did you just imagine it? Are you making too much of this? Should you just try harder? Self-doubt becomes a constant companion, whispering that maybe everyone else is right and you're the problem. The world gaslights you until you start to gaslight yourself.

Sometimes, the loneliness is so sharp it's physical. You sit in a room full of people, their laughter bouncing off the walls, and feel a thousand miles away. You watch your friends plan trips you can't join. You see your colleagues move up the ladder while you're stuck negotiating for basic accommodations. You scroll through social media and see lives unfolding with a kind of casual freedom you barely remember. And you wonder if anyone notices how much it costs you, just to keep showing up.

There is a price to not being believed, to having your reality questioned, to being erased by well-meaning policies and ignored by systems that were never built for you. The price is paid in fragments: a little autonomy here, a sliver of confidence there, a handful of dreams you quietly let go. Some days, it's all too much. Some days, the weight of being unseen is heavier than the disability itself.

So yes, this book is about telling the truth. But it's also about survival. Mine, first. Maybe yours, too. I wrote it because I needed to say the things I was never allowed to say out loud the grief, the frustration, the small joys that still manage to break through. I wrote it because I needed to believe my own story, even if no one else did.

Because until we name the cost, we'll keep paying it in silence. Until we name the loneliness, we'll keep carrying it alone. Until we name the pain, we'll keep trying to convince ourselves it's not real. This is my attempt to break that silence to put words to the things we've been told to hide, and to say, plainly: I see you. I believe you. And you are not alone, even in the moments when it feels like you are.

If you're reading this and you recognize yourself here, know that this book is for you. For the days when courage feels impossible. For the nights when the distance between you and the world seems unbridgeable. For all the times you've wondered if you're the only one. You're not. I promise.

Introduction

I've never been any good at looking away when something's wrong. Maybe it's stubbornness, maybe it's survival, or maybe it's what happens when social justice is stitched into your bones before you even know the words for it. For me, it wasn't just an idea in a textbook or a slogan on a T-shirt. It was the rhythm of my childhood—present in the background of family dinners, in the way my parents noticed and named unfairness, and in the moments that planted those seeds in me, early and deep.

I remember sitting cross-legged in Girl Scouts, a mess of construction paper and markers around me, writing letters to city officials about sidewalks that crumbled under our feet. We were supposed to be earning a civics badge, but to me it felt like a dare—a chance to say out loud that things could be better, that we didn't have to just accept what was broken. I still remember the grown-ups acting surprised that we cared so much that we really believed someone might listen to us. But I did believe it. I believed small voices could make change, even if the change started slow. That badge might be long gone, but the feeling stuck with me: if something's wrong, you say so. And if you can't fix it, you keep trying, or you find someone who will try with you.

That's how social justice took hold in me, not as a theory, but as a habit. It was watching my mom write letters to the school board about classroom resources, her pen moving with a mix of hope and frustration. It was the way my dad shrugged off tiredness to help neighbors fill out forms they couldn't read. In our house, fairness wasn't optional; it was the point. "You don't get to complain if you're not willing to do something about it," my mom said more than once, her voice sharp and loving all at once. It was a lesson I didn't realize I was learning until years later, when I found myself unable to keep quiet in rooms where silence was the norm.

So maybe it's no wonder that by the time I made it to college, the first in my family to do it, I had this radar for injustice that never shut off. I noticed who was left out, who was questioned, who got to belong without having to explain themselves. I tried to blend in, to say thank you, to keep my head down and not rock the boat. But that itch, that Girl Scout still living in my chest, never let me forget that just because something's "normal" doesn't mean it's right.

I never really pictured myself in higher education, not as a student and definitely not as a professional. Most of my early years, I spent trying to pass, hiding what made me different, pushing through pain, apologizing for needing time or help. I thought if I just worked harder, needed less, tried not to make trouble, I'd finally fit. But that's the thing about spaces that weren't built for you, they're never safe, even when you follow all the rules. Fitting in, I figured out, is about erasing your edges. Belonging is about refusing to disappear. And social justice, for me, is about refusing to stop naming what's broken, even when it would be so much easier to stay quiet.

My journey through higher education and through disability has been shaped by this constant tension: the push to hide, the pull to be seen, the bone-deep need to do what's right even when it costs me. Sometimes that looks like speaking up in meetings, sometimes it looks like writing yet another email about why access isn't optional, sometimes it's just showing up, again, when I'd rather disappear. The Girl Scout in me is still here, still writing letters—sometimes with words, sometimes just by refusing to shrink.

So, welcome. Welcome to a space where we stop pretending everything's fine. Where accommodations aren't a prize or a privilege, but a baseline. Where "need" isn't a dirty word, and where the work of justice is never done alone.

This isn't a book of easy answers or perfect stories. It's a collection of truths—mine, and maybe yours too. It's for the student who's afraid to ask for help, for the adjunct who hides his chronic pain, for the staff member who memorizes every ramp and bench but never says why. It's for anyone who's ever been praised for being "resilient" while breaking under the weight of relentless adaptation.

If you're looking for a manifesto, you won't find it here. What you will find are stories of discomfort, of heartbreak, of connection, of hope. Stories that remind us that social justice isn't something you arrive at—it's something you do, repeatedly, in big ways and small.

So come in, with your questions, your doubts, your hope, your exhaustion. Set down your mask for a minute. Imagine what could happen if we all stopped pretending, all stopped apologizing for needing a seat at the table.

Let's start, right here. Let's start, together.

1
Invisible leashes

There's a moment I return to often, though not always by choice. It's stitched into the fabric of my memory, quiet but unshakable. I'm standing just outside a classroom, one hand gripping the leash of my service dog, Lily-Rue, and the other hovering near the door handle, unsure whether to go in or turn back. From the outside, I might have looked calm, collected, maybe even confident. But inside, I was shattering, caught in a place that was both familiar and foreign.

I was physically present, yes, but emotionally, I was floating somewhere between belonging and being completely out of place. Was I there as a student eager to learn? As a university staff member quietly scanning the environment? As a disabled woman trying not to take up too much space? Or all three, collapsing into one anxious heartbeat?

At that moment, I didn't feel like I had permission to show up as all of me.

I wasn't just a student. I wasn't just a professional. I was both. And I was also someone navigating the realities of a dynamic, nonapparent disability, one that doesn't come with predictable flare-ups or refined timing. My body doesn't RSVP in advance. One minute, I can be participating in a meeting, answering emails, moving through my day like anyone else. The next, my joints dislocate. My heart races when it shouldn't. Fatigue crushes me mid-sentence.

Living with conditions like Ehlers-Danlos Syndrome and Postural Orthostatic Tachycardia Syndrome means learning to function in a state of constant unpredictability, and doing so in a world that demands consistency, proof, and poise. But there's no neat way to package or perform that kind of experience. So, I stood there, holding Lily-Rue's leash, trying to remind myself that showing up in that space wasn't a disruption. It was a declaration. I deserve to be here, even when the room wasn't built with someone like me in mind.

And yet, I still questioned it.

Should I step back and let someone else go first? Should I apologize for the space we take up, for the dog by my side, for the accommodations I need, for the way my disability refuses to stay invisible? Should I prepare a script for the questions I knew were coming?

> "Is she in training?"
> "Is she here for someone else?"
> "Oh, what a cute therapy dog!"

Every part of me wanted to walk into that classroom as my full self. But every part of me also knew what it meant to do that: vulnerability, assumptions, correction, exhaustion. All before the lecture even began. That's the weight of being both seen and misunderstood. That's the weight of standing on the threshold, not just of a classroom, but of visibility itself. In that moment, I wasn't sure which part of me had the right to enter. Was I taking up too much space? Was I going to be seen as capable or coddled? Would they assume Lily-Rue was just for comfort or attention, a kind of accessory? And the question that haunted me most: Was I even *disabled enough* to justify her presence?

It's hard to explain the mental gymnastics of constantly having to calculate your own worthiness, of wondering if your pain is visible enough, if your diagnosis is legitimate enough, if your presence is palatable enough. I didn't always call myself disabled. In fact, for a long time, I avoided the word altogether. It felt heavy, like something I hadn't earned the right to claim.

I had been raised to be independent. Capable. Helpful. My value came from doing, achieving, and performing well, on the field, on the stage, in the classroom. I was the one who got things done, the one who showed up early and stayed late, the one who didn't complain. Being an athlete and dancer reinforced that narrative. There was always applause for pushing through the pain, always praise for "toughing it out." So, I learned to smile through discomfort. To tell my body *not now* when it asked for rest. To carry my exhaustion like a badge of honor.

But the whispers from my body didn't stop. They got louder. And eventually, they turned into screams.

By the time I was diagnosed with Ehlers-Danlos Syndrome (EDS) and Postural Orthostatic Tachycardia Syndrome (POTS), I had already internalized years of doubt, my own and others. I wasn't surprised by the diagnosis. I had known something wasn't right for a long time. But knowing and accepting are two very different things. I thought I would feel relief. I thought finally having a name for my symptoms would bring clarity. Instead, I felt grief. Grief for the life I thought I could still push my way back into.

Grief for the version of me who had always relied on effort alone to compensate for pain.

Chronic illness didn't just disrupt my routine, it redefined it. Some days, I could run errands, attend meetings, and carry conversations with ease. Other days, I couldn't get out of bed without bracing myself for dizzy spells, joint dislocations, or overwhelming fatigue that made brushing my teeth feel like a marathon. I needed help. And asking for help felt like failure. Like letting go of the narrative I'd clung to my entire life: that strength meant doing it all on your own.

That's when Lily-Rue came into my life.

I didn't know how much I needed her until she was there, grounding me. Her presence was more than physical assistance. It was assurance. It was the soft, steady reminder that I wasn't broken. I just navigated the world differently. Training with her gave me things that I hadn't felt in a long time: safety, confidence, and agency. She helped me walk into places that I had started to avoid. She interrupted symptoms before they became emergencies. She gave me back parts of my life that illness had quietly stolen.

But Lily-Rue did something else too, something I wasn't fully prepared for.

She made my invisible disability… visible.

And with visibility came the questions

> "Is she in training?"
> "Is she for someone else?"
> "You don't look disabled." "You're not blind though, does she really need to go everywhere with you?"

I expected these comments from strangers at grocery stores or the occasional nosy passerby. I didn't expect them from the people I worked alongside. From colleagues in staff meetings. From supervisors. From academics who regularly touted diversity and inclusion in PowerPoint slides but flinched at the presence of my dog. That was the betrayal that I wasn't prepared for.

And what made it even more complicated was knowing that Lily-Rue is privately trained by me. In New Jersey, that's a legal right, and an essential one for people like me who don't have the $30,000 or the multi-year waitlist required for an organization-trained dog. But having a privately trained service dog adds an extra layer of pressure that people don't always see. She's incredible, but she's also an animal. A living being. Not a robot. She learns. She makes mistakes. She might sniff someone's bag, or bark once if startled. She might lick a friendly hand before I can cue her otherwise. And every time that happens, I feel the shame creep in. The sense that I must prove, again, that we belong. That she is trained. That we're "legit."

It's a strange thing, advocating for accessibility while simultaneously trying to be as invisible and unobtrusive as possible. I tried to be kind. Patient. Informative. I tried not to make people feel bad for asking, even when I was asked the same thing for the fifth time that week. I didn't want to seem "difficult" or "defensive." I wanted to be the easy employee, the flexible one, the one who wasn't a burden. But at the same time, I knew I had to hold the line, not just for myself, but for others who might not have the privilege, the language, or the job security to push back.

So, I corrected people. Kindly. But firmly.

> No, she's not in training.
> Yes, she's working.
> Yes, she needs to be here.
> No, I'm not blind, and you don't have to be to have a service dog.

It was, and still is, a balancing act. One foot in advocacy. One foot in self-preservation. I found myself navigating this tight-rope between education and exhaustion. Between grace and grit. Between wanting to belong and needing to be seen accu-rately. Because the truth is, I do take up space. And I am disabled enough. And Lily-Rue's presence isn't up for debate.

The hardest part? Knowing that the students, often first year, barely out of high school, were the ones asking thoughtful ques-tions, respecting boundaries, and adapting with kindness. It was the professional staff and faculty, those tasked with setting the tone of inclusivity, who seemed the most resistant, the most uncomfortable, the most uninformed.

And yet, those same students gave me hope. They were willing to learn. Willing to listen. Willing to advocate for others even before fully understanding what advocacy meant. They treated me, and Lily-Rue, with a kind of openness that reminded me why I still believe in higher education, even if I don't always feel believed by some of the people in it.

There's this unspoken expectation in higher education that everyone's smart enough to "get it." We're surrounded by people with advanced degrees, published articles, and framed creden-tials on their office walls, people who pride themselves on being

progressive, informed, and inclusive. But when it comes to disability and service dog etiquette, I've seen some of the most educated professionals behave with breathtaking ignorance.

The very people who speak at diversity panels, who lead strategic
planning meetings about equity and access, who proudly share
DEI hashtags on social media, these are often the same individuals who flinch when Lily-Rue walks into a room. Who whisper,
"Should she really be here?" as if I can't hear them. Or who corner
me with comments that are equal parts passive-aggressive and
performatively polite: "Well, you should've told us ahead of time,"
as though my presence with a clearly working service dog is a
disruption to be managed rather than a right to be honored.

It's not always overt. It's the silence when I enter a meeting room,
the subtle glances exchanged between colleagues. The way
people step around me and Lily-Rue like we're in the way. It's the
change in tone during a conversation when I mention that I'll
need to bring her along to a professional development event. Or
worse, the time someone casually joked, "We'll make sure there's
a corner for the dog," like we were an inconvenience instead of
attendees.

And yet, paradoxically, it's our students who continue to model
what real inclusion looks like.

They ask questions with curiosity, not condescension. They
don't pretend to have all the answers, but they show up, open,
respectful, and willing to learn. I've had students approach me
after class just to ask if Lily-Rue has a preferred side to walk on, or
how they can advocate for other students with service animals.
I've watched them gently redirect peers who tried to pet her,

"Hey, don't do that, she's working", with a casual confidence that even seasoned professionals sometimes lack.

It gives me hope. Not just for higher education, but for the future of leadership, of allyship, of human connection. Maybe change won't come from top-down policies, but from the grassroots empathy that students bring into these spaces.

Still, hope is complicated when you're living in two roles. When you're trying to stay afloat while carrying the emotional weight of systems that weren't built with you in mind.

As a student, I had a supportive experience with Accessibility Services. They knew what to ask. They didn't require me to prove myself at every turn. They helped me craft a plan that allowed me to learn, rest, and advocate without having to explain the same things repeatedly. It was one of the few spaces on campus where I felt like my disability didn't need to be justified.

But when I transitioned into my staff role at the very same university, everything shifted.

HR wanted more forms. More documentation. More justification. Policies that once protected me now felt like obstacles, used not to facilitate support, but to delay, dilute, or deny it. I was the same person, with the same diagnosis, the same dog, and the same medical documentation. But suddenly, I was seen differently. Not as a student to be supported, but as an employee to be scrutinized.

I'll never forget the meeting where I brought up the idea of updating our internal policies around service animals. I came prepared, articles, ADA guidance, case law examples. I didn't expect immediate change, but I expected conversation.

Instead, I got silence.

Then someone finally said, "Well, we've never had a problem before." As if my existence, and the barriers I was naming, were a personal inconvenience. As if silence from past employees equaled proof of equity. I left that meeting with my stomach in knots, questioning if I'd just made things worse for myself.

And that's the thing about internalized ableism; it doesn't disappear just because you know better. In some ways, it gets louder the more you understand. I'd catch myself thinking, *Am I really disabled? Do I really need to ask for this? What if they think I'm exaggerating? What if I am?*

Those thoughts don't come from nowhere. They come from years of being socialized to believe that your worth is tied to your output. That strength means not needing help. That advocacy is an act of defiance rather than survival.

They come back every time I must explain, again, that Lily-Rue is not a therapy dog. That she is privately and owner-trained, which is my right under federal and state law. That not everyone can afford or access a program-trained dog, and that the work we've put into her training is no less valid. They come back every time she makes a small mistake, sniffs a backpack, lets out a quiet bark when startled, and I feel the room tense, like I've just confirmed every doubt someone had about whether we belonged.

And that pressure isn't just unfair, it's unsustainable.

When I enter a classroom, I'm a counselor, a scholar, a mentor. But when I enter a staff meeting with Lily-Rue, I'm often reduced to a policy exception. A walking FAQ. A risk assessment. It's draining to constantly perform not just your job, but your validity. To anticipate and prevent discomfort in others, while carrying your own with grace.

Because here's the truth: professionalism in higher education often gets conflated with silence. With compliance. With smallness. But real professionalism should mean honesty. It should mean honoring difference. It should mean asking hard questions, not just about diversity in theory, but about access in practice.

And yet, I've learned to hold space for contradiction.

I've learned that it's okay to feel hurt by the ways my presence is questioned and still believe in the value of showing up. I've learned that it's okay to be tired, to be frustrated, to be angry, and still advocate with clarity, purpose, and hope. I've learned that I don't need to be palatable to be professional. I don't need to smile through every insult or minimize my needs to protect other people's comfort.

This book is my way of reclaiming space.

Of tugging on the invisible leashes, expectations, assumptions, outdated policies, and asking why they're there in the first place. Who put them there? Who do they serve? And who do they exclude?

Maybe you've been there too, on the edge of a conversation, wondering if you'll be taken seriously. Sitting at a staff table, biting your tongue. Watching others talk about access like it's theoretical, while you live it every day. Maybe your leash looks different, a chronic illness, a neurodivergent mind, a caregiving responsibility, a deep grief that hasn't found a place to rest.

If so, I hope this chapter finds you. Not with answers, but with affirmation.

What follows isn't a guidebook. It's a conversation, honest, layered, sometimes messy. It's a story about navigating academia with a body that doesn't always cooperate, and a system that rarely does. It's about what it means to occupy space while tethered to something most people can't, or won't, see.

Together, let's unravel these leashes.

Let's pull on them gently, then firmly, until we understand where they're knotted and how to loosen them. Let's make space, real space, for difference to thrive.

Not as an afterthought. Not as an accommodation. But as the foundation of something more just, more creative, more human, and more KIND.

Sometimes I wonder what would happen if we all stopped pretending. If, for a moment, nobody felt compelled to shrink their story or sand down their edges just to fit someone else's version of "professional." What if the unwritten rules of, be smaller, be quieter, be grateful for whatever access you're given, were replaced by a culture of curiosity and care?

This isn't just about disability. It's about all the ways we're taught to erase ourselves to keep the collective peace. I see it when a first-generation student apologizes for asking a "basic" question. I see it when a colleague with a heavy accent gets talked over, or when a parent in the office quietly closes Zoom so their kid's laughter won't spill into the meeting. I see it in every nervous glance, every hesitant disclosure, every moment someone calculates whether honesty is worth the fallout.

For years, I thought I was alone in that calculus. But the longer I listen the more I pay attention the more I realize how many of us are moving through institutions that weren't built to hold us. We improvise. We compensate. We code-switch and compartmentalize, trying to protect the parts of ourselves that don't fit easily on a resume or in a staff directory.

And yet, it's those very parts—our messiness, our difference, our improvisational genius—that make communities stronger. The things we're told to hide are often the things someone else needs to see to feel less alone.

I'm not naive. I know that systems don't change overnight, and belonging isn't a guarantee just because we wish for it. But I believe in the slow, stubborn work of showing up as we are, and inviting others to do the same. I believe in the power of stories—raw, unpolished, and unfinished—to open doors that policy alone cannot.

So, if you're reading this and recognizing yourself, know this: you're not too much. Your needs are not an inconvenience. Your story is not a disruption. You don't have to earn your right to exist comfortably in the spaces you inhabit.

You are allowed to take up space. You are allowed to ask for what you need. And you are allowed to dream of a world where that doesn't feel radical.

This is where we begin not with certainty, but with the willingness to loosen what binds us, and to imagine something freer, together.

Sometimes I wonder what it would look like if we stopped measuring worth by how well someone blends in, or how little they ask for. If we peeled back the layers of etiquette and expectation, what would we find? Maybe a campus where people move at different speeds, where accommodations aren't whispered about but woven into every syllabus, every staff meeting, every hallway conversation.

I think about all the invisible negotiations happening at any given moment: the student weighing whether to miss class for a doctor's appointment, the adjunct choosing between disclosing a mental health need or staying silent to protect a contract, the staff member quietly skipping lunch to make up for what they fear is "lost time" due to a flare-up. We build our days around what's allowed, what won't make waves, what won't be held against us later.

But I also think about what happens when someone cracks the door open just enough for honesty to get through. The first time I saw another staff member bring a mobility aid to work, or a professor talk openly in a department meeting about living with chronic illness, something shifted. Not just for me, but for everyone watching. Permission slips are contagious. Sometimes, living openly is an act of generosity, whether or not you mean it that way.

There's a cost to that openness, too. Vulnerability isn't always met with understanding or applause. There are days when I wish I could just exist without having to narrate my needs or translate my reality for others. But there are also days when someone pulls me aside after a meeting and quietly says, "Thank you. I didn't think I could ask for that, too."

That's why I keep coming back. Not because it's easy, or because I'm especially brave, but because I believe the story changes every time someone else feels seen. I believe there's a future where access isn't an afterthought, where difference is not only tolerated but expected, welcomed, and valued.

The leashes we unravel aren't just our own. Every tug makes it a little easier for the next person. Every conversation, every correction, every moment of visibility, it all adds up. Maybe not fast enough, and never perfectly, but enough to remind me that change is possible. That it's already happening, in small, stubborn ways.

So, if you're standing on your own threshold uncertain, exhausted, wondering if you belong, know that you don't have to do it alone. There's room here for every story, every need, every messy, beautiful reality. Let's write the next chapter together and make the room bigger for those who come after us.

Sometimes I catch myself imagining what might unfold if we all dropped the act. If, for a moment, nobody felt compelled to shrink their story or sand down their edges just to fit someone else's version of "professional." What if the unwritten rules—be smaller, be quieter, be grateful for whatever access you're given—were replaced by a culture of curiosity and care?

There's a kind of courage in simply continuing. In showing up, again and again, even when the room feels colder or smaller than it did before. I keep thinking about the quiet ways people make space for each other moving a chair without comment, leaving the door cracked open, asking "How can I help?" and really meaning it. These are small gestures, but they're not insignificant. They signal the possibility that things could be different, that institutions could learn to bend, not just ask us to.

When I walk through campus, I'm not just carrying my own story. I'm carrying the stories of every person who's ever worried they'd be seen as an inconvenience, who's ever left early or stayed silent because it felt safer. I'm carrying the hope that maybe, if we keep tugging on these leashes, the knots will loosen. That maybe, one day, there won't be a leash at all.

2
Claiming identity in academic spaces: Disability and the self

College is often described as a time of self-discovery. For many, it's the first space where we begin to ask: *Who am I? Who do I want to become?*

But those questions don't exist in a vacuum. They are asked inside residence halls and lecture classrooms, in faculty offices and shared student lounges. They take shape in the presence or absence of community. And for disabled students and professionals, those questions can quickly become more convoluted than they seem.

Disability identity isn't always something we grow up claiming. Sometimes, it's something we deny, hide, or try to outrun. Other times, it's something we feel internally but aren't ready to say out loud not because we're ashamed, but because we've seen how people react when we do.

For me, claiming the word *disabled* took time. And truthfully, I still have days when I question whether I have the "right" to it. Especially on the days when I look "fine," when I speak clearly, when I walk without a limp. Especially when people see Lily, my service dog, before they see me.

But here's what I've learned: disability identity doesn't have a timeline. It doesn't appear on a medical chart or follow a clean narrative arc. It's shambolic. It's deeply personal. And it's shaped by the places we move through and the people we encounter along the way.

At thirty-something, though, something felt undeniably different. I knew that as one gets older, everyone expects a few aches and the slow creep of fatigue, but this was something else. My body, which had always been my anchor and my avenue for joy, suddenly felt foreign. I'd been active all my life: a coach and competitive gymnast until nearly twenty-nine, a bachelor's degree in dance behind me, always in motion and always thriving on it. Movement was home. Energy and spunk were my constants.

Then, almost overnight, that certainty vanished. It wasn't a single injury or a dramatic fall, just a slow, relentless unraveling. I'd wake up already tired. I'd go to coach or teach and realize my muscles ached in ways I couldn't explain. Simple things walking upstairs, holding a plank, even laughing hard left me winded or sore. Plans I used to keep without thinking now felt daunting, and I started canceling not because I didn't want to show up, but because I couldn't trust my own body anymore.

It was confusing and, honestly, scary. I kept telling myself it was just a rough patch, maybe stress, maybe overtraining, maybe not enough sleep. But deep down, I knew: this was different. This was the start of something that didn't fit any narrative I'd ever lived before. For the first time, I felt the ground shifting beneath me. I was still me, but my body was telling a new story, one I hadn't agreed to, and one that was about to change everything I thought I knew about myself.

Navigating this new reality colored every space I entered, especially in higher education. My shifting sense of self and the questions it raised about identity and belonging became even more pronounced within the walls of academia.

Higher education can be both an incubator for identity and a mirror reflecting societal stigma, and this is true no matter your age or where you are in your academic journey. As a first-generation college student, I've felt this acutely. Whether I was a freshman trying to find my footing or a graduate student balancing professional life and disability advocacy, the cultural landscapes of higher education shaped me. They molded how I saw myself and how I believed others saw me. University isn't just about learning content. It's where many of us begin the gradual, often uncomfortable work of understanding who we are, what we carry, and where we belong.

In these spaces, identity stops being theoretical and takes on edges and urgency. For disabled students and professionals, every classroom, office, or meeting becomes a negotiation: what do I reveal, and to whom? What will it cost me to ask for what I need? The campus may promise inclusion, but daily realities like inaccessible buildings, skeptical professors, or forms that don't quite fit our lives remind us that belonging is never automatic.

Sometimes, the process is empowering. Surrounded by new ideas and diverse people, I found language for experiences I'd carried in silence. I found mentors who modeled what it could look like to claim disability with pride. I learned that I wasn't alone, that my difference could be a source of connection rather than isolation.

Other days, the work of self-discovery felt like a burden. The pressure to perform not just academically, but as the "right kind" of disabled person to be inspiring but not inconvenient, open but not too vulnerable was exhausting. In these moments, the university's promise of opportunity felt conditional, dependent on my ability to fit a narrative I didn't choose.

That's the paradox of academic spaces: they can nurture identity, but they can also magnify every insecurity and amplify every barrier. For me, learning who I was disabled, driven, deserving meant learning to navigate contradiction. It meant holding space for pride and grief, hope and frustration, all at once. And it meant realizing that my story, like so many others, didn't have to fit neatly inside someone else's expectations.

In these spaces, identity stops being an abstract concept and becomes something lived, negotiated, and sometimes, fiercely protected. For disabled students and professionals, every hallway and classroom is a test: Do I disclose my needs today? Will I have to justify my presence, my accommodations, my very right to be here? There's a constant calculation how much of myself do I reveal, and what do I risk if I do?

At times, higher education offers a rare kind of liberation. Surrounded by new ideas and unfamiliar faces, I found the freedom to question old assumptions and try on new language for who I was becoming. I discovered pockets of community students and colleagues who didn't flinch at the word "disabled," who listened, who shared their own stories, who helped me imagine a future where I could be both ambitious and honest about my limitations.

But there were other days when campus felt less like a home and more like a proving ground. The weight of being "the only one" in a seminar, or the unspoken expectation to represent all disabled people, could be suffocating. I learned to brace myself for skepticism in office hours, for raised eyebrows when I asked about accessibility, for the well-meaning "You're so inspiring!" that often carried an undercurrent of disbelief.

The paradox is this: higher education promises transformation, but it often resists the very changes it asks of its students. It celebrates individuality in theory, but conformity in practice. If you don't match the invisible template if your needs are inconvenient, if your difference is visible you are reminded, sometimes subtly and sometimes not, that full belonging is still conditional.

Yet amid all this, I kept searching for a place to land. I kept trying to carve out a space where my disabled self wasn't something to apologize for, but something I could claim with pride. That search is ongoing. It's messy. It's full of setbacks and small victories. But every time I choose honesty over hiding, every time I connect with someone else navigating the same contradictions, I feel a little less alone. And that, I'm learning, is a kind of belonging too.

Becoming disabled, or realizing you are

There's a phrase in the disability community: *coming out as disabled.*

It may sound strange at first, but for many of us, it's real. Sometimes, we spend years downplaying our symptoms, pushing through pain, laughing off our limitations. We tell ourselves it's not "that bad," that other people have it worse. We become masters of masking. Of performing wellness. Of passing. We pass as though we're healthy. As though we can operate just as efficiently, just as consistently, just as flawlessly as everyone else. We convince ourselves that we don't need accommodations, don't need considerations, don't need to take up space. We strive to be seen as reliable, dependable, high performing, all the things disability is assumed to take away from you. And in doing so, we silence parts of ourselves that are asking to be heard.

We get good at pretending. At pushing through. At becoming exactly what the system demands of us: easy, efficient, unquestioning. We smile when we're in pain. We say "I'm fine" when our bodies are screaming. We internalize the idea that to be respected, we must be unbroken or at least look that way. The world rewards us for disappearing our needs, so we learn to disappear them ourselves.

But there's a cost. There is always a cost.

The effort it takes to keep up the performance to meet every deadline, to show up to every meeting, to answer every email with cheerful precision is immense. And when we finally break, when our bodies crash or our mental health falters, the system doesn't ask why we had to push that hard. It asks why we didn't say anything sooner. Why we didn't ask for help. Why we weren't "proactive."

But how can you ask for help in a workplace that praises invisibility? How do you disclose a need when you've been rewarded for hiding it? How do you say "I can't keep going like this" when you've been the one everyone relies on to keep going no matter what?

Eventually, the mask slips. Not because we want it to, but because we can't hold it up anymore. The pain gets louder. The symptoms get harder to manage.

The anxiety creeps in and settles into our bones. And with it comes fear … fear of being seen, not as high-functioning or exceptional, but as fragile, inconsistent, inconvenient.

But here's what I've learned: fragility is not failure. Needing support is not weakness. And coming undone is sometimes the most honest thing we can do.

Reclaiming disability means shedding the performance. It means unlearning the shame. It means admitting, out loud, that we're not okay not because we've done something wrong, but because we've spent years surviving systems that were never designed with us in mind.

Upon saying it once we speak that truth, we begin to make space. Space for accommodations. Space for community. Space for rest. Space for wholeness. Because we were never meant to live in pieces.

I didn't start using the word *disabled* because someone told me to. I began using it because my body and my circumstances kept colliding with systems that didn't see me. I used it after missing too many opportunities, after leaving too many spaces that weren't built with me in mind. And once I said it out loud, it stuck because it finally made sense.

But just as I was learning to claim that identity, I was reminded how fragile it is to be seen.

The paradox is this: higher education promises transformation, but it often resists the very changes it asks of its students. It celebrates individuality in theory, but conformity in practice. If you don't match the invisible template, if your needs are inconvenient, if your difference is visible you are reminded, sometimes subtly and sometimes not, that full belonging is still conditional.

Yet amid all this, I kept searching for a place to land. I kept trying to carve out a space where my disabled self wasn't something to apologize for, but something I could claim with pride. That search is ongoing. It's messy. It's full of setbacks and small victories. But every time I choose honesty over hiding, every time I connect with someone else navigating the same contradictions, I feel a little less alone. And that, I'm learning, is a kind of belonging too.

It's important to recognize, too, that there isn't just one way to enter the world of disability. There are at least two distinct cultures: those born disabled and those who become disabled later in life. Each brings its own history, its own set of survival tactics, and its own relationship to the world.

For many who are born disabled, the reality that the world wasn't built for them is a foundational truth. They grow up attuned to barriers physical, social, and attitudinal and learn early on how to navigate or resist them. Their communities, their humor, and their sense of self are often shaped by a kind of resourceful resilience. There's a deep understanding, sometimes unspoken, that adaptation is a daily necessity, and that "normal" is a moving target set by others.

For those of us who become disabled, the journey is different. We start out with a certain kind of privilege moving through a world that, for the most part, was designed with us in mind. When that changes, it's disorienting. There's a grieving process, not just for lost abilities but for the ease of unthinking participation in everyday life. Ramps and elevators that were once invisible suddenly become lifelines. Invitations now come with mental calculations: Will I be able to attend? Will I be able to keep up? There's a sense of loss, sometimes even shame, in realizing how much we took for granted.

The emotional terrain here is complicated. There's often guilt … Guilt for not understanding before, guilt for needing help now, guilt for occupying space in a community you didn't always see. There's anger, too: at your own body, at inaccessible systems, at the ignorance or insensitivity of others. And beneath it all, there's a slow recalibration of identity. Who am I now? What parts of my old self can I keep? What must I let go?

Both experiences being born disabled or becoming disabled come with their own forms of wisdom and pain. Those born into disability may carry the exhaustion of always having to fight, but also the pride of a culture that is vibrant and creative. Those who become disabled bring the shock of transition, but also the insight that comes from seeing the world through new eyes. Both contribute to the richness and complexity of disabled community. And both are valid, necessary stories as we work to claim our place in spaces that weren't built for any of us.

The incident

There was an incident. One that began quietly but unraveled quickly.

I was walking through the student center, just passing through at the same time a university-sponsored pet therapy event was being held. I didn't stop. I didn't engage. I was simply in a shared space, doing my job, with Lily by my side. But what followed was a chain of emails, policies, and whispers I wasn't prepared for.

I received a message informing me that Lily had been reported as "aggressive" toward a child. The claim had come to the sender fourth-hand. No names. No formal complaint. Just a vague account. I was reminded of the university's ten-foot distance policy between service dogs and pet therapy animals. I was told that Lily must always be tethered to an object if I wasn't holding her leash. I was asked again if Lily had completed her training.

She had. She is a fully trained medical alert and mobility service dog. ADA compliant. Responsive only to me. But in that moment, her training didn't seem to matter. My documentation didn't matter. I didn't matter.

The trauma of that moment reverberated for weeks. Lily regressed in her training. I began avoiding the student center. The anxiety of simply being in shared spaces of doing my job while navigating silent judgment became overwhelming.

I later wrote:

> "While I will continue to respect the agreement and maintain the necessary ten-foot distance in applicable situations, I cannot guarantee that I will not be present in the student center or other areas where pet therapy may take place. My presence in shared spaces is not something I can always predict or avoid.

The situation was quite traumatic and unfortunately set Lily back several weeks in her training. Additionally, the anxiety I've experienced as a result has been significant. I need pet therapy and those coordinating it to fully understand the rights I have as a service dog handler.

I would also like clarification: Are other students and staff treated in the same manner, or is this being uniquely applied to me?"

I never received a clear answer.

What that email didn't capture and what policies never seem to capture is the toll it took on me. Not just professionally, but mentally, emotionally, and physically. In the days and weeks that followed, I lived in a constant state of hypervigilance. Every time I walked through a public space, I scanned the room for who might be watching, who might report us next, who might misunderstand a simple moment and turn it into another accusation. My heart raced in places that used to feel routine. Meetings became draining. Casual hallway interactions felt dangerous. I couldn't focus. I couldn't breathe deeply. The tension never left my shoulders.

I started avoiding spaces I once moved through freely not because I had done anything wrong, but because I was afraid of being wrongfully scrutinized again. The anxiety wasn't mild or manageable. It spiraled. I began waking up already tired, already bracing for the day. I lost my appetite. I cried on my way to work. I stopped taking breaks because stepping outside my office felt risky. My body absorbed the stress, and my medical symptoms intensified. Eventually, I had to be medicated for the anxiety that had grown loud enough to interfere with every part of my day.

This wasn't just discomfort. It was a psychological wound that kept reopening every time I was asked to "just explain again" why Lily was with me. Every time I was subtly or overtly treated like a liability instead of a colleague. The pressure to remain calm, composed, and professional while being silently targeted was unbearable. And the silence that followed my response—no resolution, no accountability, no assurance was deafening. It confirmed what I feared most: that I was being singled out, and that no one was going to stop it.

What happened wasn't just an "incident." It was a fracture. One that reshaped my relationship with my workplace, my colleagues, and my sense of safety. It taught me, painfully, that even in a space that champions inclusion on paper, the burden of proof of presence, of legitimacy, of belonging still falls disproportionately on disabled bodies.

In the aftermath, I found myself rewriting reality just to survive it. Maybe it wasn't that serious. Maybe I'm overreacting. Maybe if I just stay quiet, it'll go away. That's the dangerous thing about institutional gaslighting. It doesn't just make you doubt the system; it also makes you doubt yourself. I started walking on eggshells, carefully calculating every movement Lily made. Was she too close to someone? Did she sit in the wrong spot? Would her tail touching someone's shoe trigger another complaint? Every mundane interaction was filtered through the lens of imagined punishment.

And still, I was expected to function. To lead. To support students. To keep smiling in meetings. The labor didn't pause just because I was unraveling. In fact, the performance of normalcy only intensified. Because in academia, distress is only acceptable when it's quiet. Disability is only respected when it's compliant. I felt the walls closing in, not just around my body, but around my voice. The message was clear: stay small, stay silent, stay grateful for what little access you've been allowed.

But I couldn't stay silent. I wouldn't. Because silence, for me, has always been more painful than truth.

So, I documented everything. I reread the ADA guidance. I pulled policies, archived emails, reviewed past accommodations. I reminded myself daily, that I was not the problem. That my presence was not a disruption. That my right to access didn't end where someone else's discomfort began.

Still, it broke something in me. Not permanently. But undeniably.

My trust in the institution fractured. My sense of safety at work cracked. My relationship with shared spaces, student centers, hallways, events changed. I no longer walked through campus as a professional contributing to the academic community. I walked through it as a potential target, trying to prove I belonged in a place I'd already earned.

And Lily? She felt it too. Her behavior shifted. Her alerting became more hesitant. Her body tensed near the same doorways I once breezed through. My dog, trained to respond to the subtle shifts in my body, now reflected the emotional damage this experience caused. Her regression wasn't about her training it was about her environment. About the emotional residue we were both forced to carry.

What happened wasn't an isolated misunderstanding. It was a manifestation of institutional ableism, quiet, indirect, and deeply embedded. It reminded me that in higher education, access often hinges not on policy, but on perception. And perception is shaped by bias, by ignorance, by discomfort with anything or anyone that doesn't fit the norm.

But despite it all, I'm still here. And that is no small thing.

Surviving that ordeal changed me. It forced me to reckon with how fragile safety and belonging can be for disabled people in spaces that claim to be inclusive. I learned that resilience isn't just about enduring hardship. It's about refusing to let other people's projections define your reality. Every day I chose to show up was an act of resistance, even when showing up meant moving through fear or exhaustion.

But the truth is, no one should have to summon that much courage just to do their job. The emotional and physical labor of self-advocacy, of constantly having to prove your legitimacy, is its own kind of invisible work. It's work that rarely gets acknowledged, that doesn't show up on performance reviews, but it's as real as any meeting or deadline.

What happened with Lily was a personal breaking point, but it was also a window into a larger pattern. A reminder that ableism is baked into policy, into perception, into the very architecture of campus life. The lesson is as exhausting as it is clear: access is not a one-time achievement, but a daily negotiation.

And yet, I remain. Not just out of stubbornness, but out of hope. Hope that by refusing to shrink, by refusing to be silent, I might help carve out a little more space for those who come after me. My story is not unique, and that's exactly why it needs to be told. Because every time we name the harm, every time we refuse to disappear, we push the boundaries of what inclusion can really mean.

If you're reading this and recognizing yourself in these words, know that you're not alone. The burden is heavy, but it shouldn't be yours to carry in silence. And maybe, as more of us speak, the silence itself will finally begin to crack.

The labor of belonging: Navigating visibility, doubt, and daily resistance

In these academic spaces, identity stops being something theoretical and becomes a series of lived decisions. For disabled students and professionals, every day is filled with small negotiations: Should I disclose my needs today? Is it safer to mask my pain or to be open about it? Will my accommodations be met with understanding or suspicion? Even the simplest routines where to sit in a classroom, how to navigate a crowded hallway, whether to attend a campus event can become weighted with calculation and second-guessing.

Sometimes, higher education offers a rare kind of liberation. It can be a place where new language and perspectives help us understand ourselves in ways we never could before. I found comfort in discovering peers who spoke openly about disability, who didn't flinch at words like "chronic illness" or "access needs." Those moments of connection were a relief a reminder that I wasn't alone in what I carried.

But often, the work of claiming identity here is lonely and exhausting. The pressure to fit in, to meet expectations, to represent not just myself but an entire community, can be overwhelming. I learned quickly that it's possible to feel both hyper-visible and completely unseen. Some days, it felt as though my disability was all anyone could see; other days, it was erased so thoroughly that my needs disappeared right along with it.

What I've come to understand is that the journey to claiming identity isn't a straight line. It's a messy, nonlinear process that's shaped by every space we enter and every interaction we have. Some days, I move through campus with confidence and pride. Other days, I carry the weight of self-doubt, the sting of microaggressions, the ache of being misunderstood.

Still, I keep showing up. I keep reaching for community, for language, for spaces that allow all of me to exist. Because if there's one thing higher education has taught me, it's that who we are is always in motion shaped by the questions we dare to ask, the stories we share, and the people we choose to become.

The weight of being seen

That experience was more than a policy reminder. It was a message: *You don't belong here.*

Not just me, but what I represent. Disability. Disruption. Complexity.

And that's when I fully understood that I am not just navigating my own identity. I am navigating how my presence challenges others' expectations. People didn't see me as a professional, or a doctoral student, or an educator. They saw my dog. My difference. My inconvenience.

In those moments, I didn't feel empowered. I felt like a spectacle.

Huge events with lots of people make me feel like I must accommodate everyone around me. Like I need to shrink myself, minimize my presence, and make sure Lily doesn't draw attention. That's what ableism does. It teaches us to take up less space.

But invisibility is a heavy thing to carry.

The role of environment

Disability identity doesn't exist in isolation (Anderson, n.d.) It lives in context. It breathes and shifts depending on where we are, who we're with, and how we're treated. It is shaped in the waiting rooms where we rehearse how to explain our needs one more time without sounding "difficult." It takes form in the lecture halls where our requests for flexibility are met with understanding, or with skepticism. It grows in moments of solidarity and shrinks under the weight of silence. It is carried in our bodies but built in community.

It lives in the policy memos that never quite reflect the lived experience of navigating campus as a disabled person experiences. Like the therapy dog incident that I described above, when simply passing through a student center with my service dog led to whispered accusations and a chain of policy reminders that left me feeling scrutinized and unsafe. Lived experience, in this context, means enduring the anxiety that follows being reported without warning or evidence, the exhaustion of repeatedly justifying your presence, and the way your confidence in public spaces can be shattered by a single misunderstanding. It's found in the accessibility statements buried at the bottom of syllabi, in the hallway glances when someone notices your service dog and hesitates to ask why. It is shaped by the tone of a professor's voice when you ask for an extension, by the sigh of a colleague when you mention needing time off for a medical appointment, by the student who looks at your cane or your headphones or your need and simply says, "Oh. I didn't know."

A student might feel empowered in a disability cultural center, surrounded by peers who speak the same unspoken language of navigating ableism. They might feel seen for the first time, affirmed in the fullness of who they are. But then, in the next class, they might sit in the back corner, alone, the only one requesting accommodations, hyper-aware of the professor's reluctance or the classmate's side-eye. One moment they're included. The next they're invisible.

A staff member might be publicly praised for their strength, admired for their "perseverance," and quietly labeled "too complicated" when they request flexible scheduling or assistive technology. The praise feels hollow when it comes without real support.

Their identity is both celebrated and contained, recognized just enough to appear inclusive, but not enough to change systems.

A faculty member might stand at the front of the room, lecturing on inclusive pedagogy, advocating for universal design, encouraging students to bring their whole selves into the learning environment. But that same faculty member might be silently masking their own neurodivergence, carefully managing chronic illness behind office doors, afraid that disclosing their own disability would undermine their authority or credibility. So, they keep it hidden. They become an advocate for others, but not for themselves.

And me? I'm all three. Staff. Student. Educator. I live in the liminal space between them, carrying the weight of each role while navigating the friction of their contradictions. I see it from every angle. And what I've learned, what I continue to learn, is that even the most well-meaning, inclusive campuses can have blind spots. Especially when policies are applied inconsistently, interpreted without empathy, or used as shields rather than starting points for conversation.

The truth is, you can have a strong policy and still harm people. You can have an ADA statement on your website and still exclude students. You can have diversity programming without ever mentioning disability. You can advocate for accessibility in the abstract and still fail to support the people living it every day.

Disability identity lives in the details. In the pauses. In the inconsistencies. In the way someone looks at you when you say, "I need help." It is in the unspoken rules we learn to navigate. And until those rules are challenged, until we build campuses that reflect all our realities, our identities will remain something we are forced to explain, defend, and protect, rather than something we are invited to claim with pride.

There are days I miss who I used to be, or more precisely, who I thought I was before illness rewrote the blueprint. Disability didn't just arrive as a medical reality; it reshaped how I moved through the world and how the world moved around me. My mental health and my physical disability don't exist in isolation; they coexist, sometimes in harmony, often in tension. And while I've come to understand disability as a culture, not a curse, the grief of change lingers. Becoming disabled later in life wasn't just a diagnosis it was a cultural shift, a reshaping of identity. Makeup and a carefully chosen outfit might give the appearance of health, but wellness cannot be measured by aesthetics. I've learned that chronic pain doesn't clock out, that productivity must be reimagined, and that quiet work can still yield loud results. I've also come to realize that a strong sense of social justice is not always met with applause. It can be isolating especially when you're the only one in the room questioning a system everyone else is trying to protect. The academic world thrives on performance, and ableism is often baked into its architecture, policies, and assumptions. As a disabled person in higher education, I've come to understand that exclusion doesn't always announce itself through closed doors. It often shows up in stairs instead of ramps, in "yes, you can attend" paired with inaccessible formats, in "we're flexible" accompanied by rigid approval processes. I've stood in rooms that called themselves inclusive, only to be reminded through subtle glances and overlooked needs that access, while not explicitly denied, was quietly made impossible.

The internalized confusion that follows is exhausting too disabled for some rooms, not disabled enough for others; too competent to need help, too needy to be believed. Navigating these contradictions is part of what it means to live with a dynamic disability. And through it all, I trust my resilience to carry me. But I also know that no one should have to constantly prove their pain or package their needs to be palatable. We shouldn't have to disclose our trauma to be treated with compassion. And yet, we do because the world is still learning how to listen.

Community, intersectionality, and belonging

What makes the difference, what truly shifts the trajectory of disability identity development, is community.

It doesn't have to be a large one. Sometimes, it's just one person. One peer. One mentor. One faculty member who doesn't flinch when you say you're disabled. One person who listens without judgment, who sees you without needing an explanation, who says, "You're not alone. I've been there too."

That kind of connection can be life changing.

It changes how we see ourselves. It softens the self-doubt. It interrupts the isolation we've grown used to carrying. It gives us new language for what we've experienced in silence language that validates our pain, our pride, our complexity. Language that reminds us of our needs are not a burden, and our presence is not a disruption. When we see someone else living openly and unapologetically as disabled, it can flip a switch inside us. Suddenly, what felt shameful feels shareable. What felt like a secret becomes a story we are allowed to tell.

But not everyone finds that community easily. And for those of us who hold multiple marginalized identities disabled and Black, disabled and trans, disabled and first-generation the journey toward claiming identity becomes even more layered. We don't get to enter spaces with just one story. We carry several, all at once. We carry histories of exclusion from many directions.

We navigate campuses where the disability center doesn't reflect our culture, where the LGBTQ+ office doesn't talk about chronic illness, where first-gen programs assume we're abled, and where race-based initiatives forget that some of us are navigating both racialized and medicalized systems of oppression. We move through places that expect us to show up fully but don't always make room for our full selves.

We carry overlapping stigmas. We are told, sometimes directly and sometimes through omission, that we don't quite fit the narrative. We're too much. Too complex. Too inconvenient for neat boxes. So, we're left out. Left behind.

Or left to fend for ourselves.

And still, we fight to be seen. To be supported. To be believed.

Because for those of us living at the intersection of multiple identities, community is not just helpful. It's vital. It's what keeps us from giving up. It's what reminds us that we're not anomalies, we're not asking for too much, and we're not alone (Anderson, n.d.).

When community exists, identity has room to breathe. It has room to grow. It becomes something we don't just carry quietly, but something we can name out loud with courage, with clarity, and eventually, with pride.

3
Living
in survival mode

Disability isn't just a medical diagnosis or a list of symptoms. It's a slow, grinding war that plays out every damn day inside your body, inside your mind, inside your soul. It's the kind of exhaustion that no amount of sleep can fix. The kind of pain that steals the breath from your lungs and leaves you gasping in silence. It's waking up every morning knowing that the body you live in will betray you again, and again, and again.

Living with chronic illness means living on the edge of overwhelm, every moment a balancing act between survival and surrender. Your mind is a battlefield where anxiety claws relentlessly at the edges worrying about what flare might come next, if you'll make it through the day, if you'll ever be believed when you say you're hurting. The fear isn't just physical; it's existential. It's the terror of becoming invisible, irrelevant, a burden that everyone is quietly hoping will just disappear.

And that anxiety? It's a constant scream in your head that never fully quiets. It twists your thoughts into knots. It convinces you you're too much. Too weak. Too broken. It makes every social interaction a minefield you rehearse your words, monitor your body, try to mask the tremors and exhaustion so no one notices.

Because if they notice, they might question you. They might judge you. They might decide your pain isn't real.

Depression doesn't just knock it settles in like a shadow that saps your hope and steals your joy. It wraps you in numbness, so even the things you used to love feel like distant memories. And you grieve. You grieve the life you thought you'd have, the dreams that slip through your fingers, the simple things you can't do anymore without paying a steep price. But grief doesn't come with a timeline. It's a constant companion, whispering that you're losing yourself.

Physical pain is relentless. It doesn't care if you have a meeting, or a birthday party, or a single moment of peace. It crashes over you like a wave, unpredictable and unforgiving. You get used to the ache, the stabbing, the burning, but it never stops surprising you with new ways to hurt. Each flare leaves you weaker, more fragile. You start counting the energy you have left in a day, often thinking in terms of "spoons"—a metaphor used by many people with chronic illnesses to describe limited daily energy and capacity for tasks. In this framework, each activity costs a certain number of "spoons," and when you run out, you have nothing left to give (Miserandino, 2003). Some days, you run out halfway through breakfast.

And the support you need? It's never just a quick fix. You're in a maze of doctors who sometimes listen and sometimes don't. You navigate a healthcare system that can feel indifferent or outright hostile. Mental health professionals become lifelines sometimes the only thing standing between you and the abyss. But even then, the help is patchy, the wait times long, the understanding limited.

Advocating for yourself while you're sick is an act of sheer willpower. You have to find a voice when your throat is tight with pain. You have to fight for accommodations when your energy is drained. You have to explain, again and again, that your disability is real, that your needs are valid, that you deserve dignity. And sometimes, no matter how hard you try, you're met with skepticism, disbelief, or outright dismissal.

Masking the exhausting, soul-draining performance of pretending you're "fine "becomes your survival skill. You learn to smile through tears, to laugh through exhaustion, to nod through pain. You become an expert at hiding what's really happening inside, because the world doesn't want to see your struggle. It wants you to be brave, or at least invisible.

But beneath that mask is a person fighting a war nobody asked for—a war that steals your time, your energy, your identity. The cost of disability isn't just physical. It's mental. It's emotional. It's the constant, crushing weight of survival.

There are days when I feel like I should be able to do so much. Teach full college courses. Write a dissertation that matters. Work full-time and still have the energy to fight for change in advocacy spaces. To have free time—real free time—to breathe, to laugh, to just enjoy life without counting every ounce of energy I have left.

But most days, that feels like a cruel joke.

My body betrays me in ways no one sees. It's not just fatigue it's a weight that sinks into my bones, a fog that clouds my mind, a heaviness that pins me down. Weekends, when I should be recharging, are often spent bed-rotting—staring at the ceiling, wishing I had the will to move, to get up, to do anything that might feel like progress.

Task paralysis is a thief. It creeps in silently, turning simple decisions into mountains that I don't have the strength to climb. I'll sit with a list of things to do, feel the crushing pressure, and then do nothing at all. It's not laziness. It's not a lack of desire. It's the overwhelming weight of mental exhaustion, the kind that smothers motivation before it even has a chance to spark.

My mental health? It often feels nonexistent. It's swallowed by the constant fight to just survive physically and emotionally. Anxiety and depression don't take breaks. They settle in, like unwelcome roommates who refuse to leave, whispering doubts, amplifying fears, stealing hope. I'm fighting battles on so many fronts that sometimes I don't recognize myself anymore.

I want to do more. I want to be more. But my body and mind have limits that don't respect my ambitions. And that's one of the hardest truths I live with every day.

This isn't a story of giving up. It's a story of survival. Of pushing through the fog, the pain, the isolation. Of finding courage in the smallest victories, a sentence written, a class taught, a moment of connection. It's about learning to live with limits while still dreaming beyond them.

And maybe, if I'm lucky, it's about finding peace with the tension between the two.

If you're reading this and you know this fight, know this: you are not weak. You are not alone. The cost is unbearable sometimes, but your courage, just your courage is profound. And that courage, raw and real, is enough to keep you breathing, keep you fighting, keep you here.

4
Learning from the experiences of others

There's a shift that happens when you stop navigating disability alone and start finding others who are walking similar paths. This chapter explores how connecting with other disabled students, both within my own institution and across professional spaces like LinkedIn, has expanded my understanding of access, advocacy, and the layered institutional barriers that so many of us face in higher education. These connections didn't come from formal training or structured mentorship programs; they came from message threads, social media groups, comment sections, and late-night conversations that left me feeling seen in ways policy documents never could.

Through these stories, of students advocating for service dog access, managing dynamic and nonapparent disabilities, or reimagining what accommodations could look like in rigid academic environments, I began to see the bigger picture. Cross-campus dialogue revealed patterns of exclusion that felt eerily familiar, but it also uncovered creative acts of resistance and collective wisdom. What emerged was a sense of community-driven learning, the kind that transcends institutional silos and invites all of us to reimagine what equity and inclusion can truly mean when shaped by those who live it every day.

I used to think I was the only one. Not really, but it felt like that. I thought maybe I was the only student, the only higher education professional, the only employee silently navigating the weight of a disability while trying to keep up appearances in the classroom, in meetings, at the front of the room, or behind a desk.

I thought maybe I was the only one who timed bathroom breaks around class sessions because of a medical condition no one could see. The only one who drafted email after email to ask for flexibility, only to delete them out of fear of sounding "needy." The only one who avoided certain buildings not because they were too far, but because the walk would leave me dizzy, exhausted, or in pain. The only one who felt a twinge of anxiety every time someone looked at my service dog and then looked back at me, confused, curious, or skeptical.

I *knew* I wasn't the only one. But the systems we move through have a way of making you feel like you are.

Like maybe everyone else is handling things just fine. Like maybe you're just not trying hard enough. Like maybe if you could just push a little more, smile a little wider, stay a little quieter, no one would notice how hard you're working to hold everything together.

That's the illusion that isolation creates. And for a long time, I believed it.

That belief began to shift when I stumbled into a late-night Facebook group for disabled students in higher ed. I was scrolling through my phone in bed, my legs aching, the low buzz of dizziness still lingering from the day. I found a post that stopped me. A student asking, "Has anyone else had to explain for the *fifth* time this semester why they have a service dog and no, it's not for anxiety, and no, you can't pet them?"

That post had hundreds of comments.

I read every one.

They weren't all exactly like me. But they were close enough. Students with dogs named Radar and Waffles and Max, talking about lab placements, rude classmates, professors who "forgot" their accommodations. Students from state schools and Ivy Leagues, from small liberal arts colleges and massive public universities. Students in wheelchairs, with canes, with insulin pumps and hearing aids and migraines and medical conditions they were still trying to name.

That post led to another, and another. A student who couldn't get housing because the dorm didn't allow dogs, even service dogs. Another was told her cardiac alert dog would be a "distraction" in the simulation lab. One who was encouraged to withdraw from a field placement because of "insurance concerns."

But it wasn't just the exclusion that stood out. It was the ingenuity. The fire. The refusal to disappear.

One student shared how she had built a laminated card explaining the ADA's stance on service dogs to hand out when approached in public. Another had created a Google doc compiling accessibility reviews of buildings on campus not just ramps, but where the elevators broke down regularly, where the accessible bathrooms were usable. Others shared templates for accommodation request emails, scripts for meetings with disability services, even advocacy toolkits tailored to different majors.

It was then that I realized I wasn't just learning how to advocate for myself. I was learning how *we* advocate for each other.

Around that same time, I came across the story of Joey Ramp. It was sent to me by a friend who simply wrote, "You need to see this."

Joey was a neuroscience student at the University of Illinois. After a horseback riding accident that resulted in traumatic brain injury and PTSD, she returned to school with Sampson, her service dog. She was rebuilding her life. But when she reached the point in her program where she needed to complete lab work, the university told her no. Sampson wasn't allowed in the lab. It wasn't safe, they said. Her options were simple: leave him or leave the program.

She chose neither.

Instead, Joey advocated for herself. She educated university officials about federal disability law and worked directly with the U.S. Department of Justice to assert her rights. She firmly rejected the idea that access to scientific education should require sacrificing her legally protected accommodations. Her advocacy not only allowed her to remain in her program but also sparked broader conversations and policy shifts regarding service animals in hands-on academic settings nationwide. Her story was featured in *Science* magazine, highlighting the national implications of her case (Wadman, 2024).

Reading about Joey didn't just move me. It fortified me. I printed her story and kept it in my binder for a long time. I carried it into meetings where I was asked, again, why Lily needed to be in the classroom. Why she couldn't wait outside. Why I couldn't "just take a break instead."

Because sometimes, you need more than your own voice. You need the weight of someone else's fight to stand your ground.

As my network grew, so did my courage. I connected with students on LinkedIn who shared posts about their service dogs in internship interviews, who created accessibility audit tools for their departments, who were writing theses about disability justice and representation. I saw how many of us were piecing together the same puzzle in different corners of academia.

Each story carried a lesson: not just in how to survive these systems, but in how to change them.

There was Ari, a trans nonbinary student in a veterinary program who used a psychiatric service dog for dissociation and medical alert. They shared with me how isolating it was to be both queer and disabled in a program that barely acknowledged either identity. One of their professors refused to let them bring their dog into a clinical setting, claiming it would make the animals they worked with "unpredictable."

"I'm the one who becomes unpredictable when I don't have him," Ari told me. "That's the point."

Ari eventually found a workaround. They partnered with another professor who understood, adjusted their rotation, and documented everything. They now mentor younger students entering the program with service animals.

And there was Shana, a public health student living with Ehlers-Danlos Syndrome, who had to petition three separate departments to allow her to take her courses remotely on flare-up days. When she succeeded, she wrote up a step-by-step guide and posted it in her university's student group.

"I figured if I had to fight this hard," she said, "maybe I could make it a little easier for the next person."

And that's the thread that ties all of us together: not just survival, but legacy. We don't want to just get through. We want to leave the door open behind us.

When I look back on the hardest days of my academic life, the moments I almost gave up weren't because of my disability. They were because of the loneliness that came with it. The meetings where I was talked over. The silence in response to my disclosures. The questioning glances when I brought Lily into a new space.

What pulled me through wasn't just grit. It was community. It was someone saying, "I've been there too. Here's what helped."

We are rewriting the narrative of what it means to be a student, a scholar, a professional with a disability. We're showing up, even when we're not invited. We're claiming space, even when that space was never meant for us. And we're doing it together.

Because that's what makes the difference. Not just the policies, not just the paperwork. But the people who say, "You don't have to go through this alone." And once you know that it changes everything.

Common challenges faced by students with service dogs

Table 1 below highlights everyday barriers that students with service dogs often run into on college campuses. These examples are based on stories shared in conversations, social media groups, and peer networks. While they aren't pulled from a formal study, they show just how often disabled students face pushback-not because of their abilities, but because of outdated policies, lack of understanding, or inconsistent support.

These aren't one-off complaints—they're patterns. And when you hear these stories repeatedly, you begin to see the real problem isn't the dog. It's the system. Students aren't asking for special treatment. They're asking to be included in the same educational experience everyone else gets.

By understanding these challenges more clearly, we can all do better: educators, classmates, administrators. This chapter and the stories within it are a reminder that change doesn't start with policy alone. It starts with listening.

Table 1. Common barriers faced by students using service animals in experiential learning settings

Challenge	What It Can Look Like	How Often It Happens (Anecdotal)	Where the Problem Comes From
Denied Access in Labs/ Clinicals	Told the service dog can't enter a lab due to "safety issues"	Common in science and health fields	Lab safety rules not updated for access
Housing Issues	Dorm staff unsure about service dog rules; extra paperwork requested unfairly	Frequent among first-year students	Lack of staff training on ADA rights
Faculty Pushback	Professor questions if a dog is really needed or suggests alternative options	Happens often	Misunderstanding of legal and medical needs
Placement/ Internship Barriers	Told they can't bring their dog to a teaching, nursing, or social work site	Common in hands-on programs	Liability fears and unclear field guidelines

Challenge	What It Can Look Like	How Often It Happens (Anecdotal)	Where the Problem Comes From
Peer Reactions	Classmates pet the dog, ask invasive questions, or avoid working with the student	Regularly mentioned	Gaps in student awareness or etiquette
Trans-portation Trouble	Campus shuttles won't allow service dogs or don't know how to help	Sometimes noted	Unclear or outdated campus transportation rules
Inconsistent Accom-modation Steps	Different rules or processes depending on the office or person involved	Happens frequently	Disconnected departments and unclear policies
Feeling Alone or Scrutinized	Students feel judged, watched, or like they must constantly explain themselves	Nearly all report this experience	Campus culture and ongoing ableism

5
The cost
of disclosure

Disclosing a disability in higher education is never just a paper-work process. It's not a box to check or a form to upload. It's a moment of deep vulnerability that can shape the rest of your experience in that space.

For me, it started quietly. A hallway conversation. A one-on-one meeting with my supervisor. The kind of disclosure that isn't planned, but necessary. I needed accommodations, but more than that, I needed understanding. And what I got in return wasn't always either.

Sometimes, the response was cautious support, wrapped in hesitation. Sometimes, it was defensiveness, masked as confusion. Most times, it came with a heavy silence. And almost always, it came with conditions. I had to prove I really needed what I was asking for. I had to manage the discomfort of others. I had to be polite about it. Not too loud. Not too persistent.

In meetings, I'd mention chronic fatigue or brain fog and watch people shift in their seats. I learned quickly that if I looked okay, I was expected to be okay. That's the invisible weight of a nonapparent disability. You're constantly defending something people can't see.

Even when I did disclose, I was often met with the same response: "But you already have your service dog." As if Lily was a cure. As if her presence alone solved everything.

She doesn't take away my joint pain. She doesn't make my dizziness vanish. She can't fight the overwhelming fatigue that sometimes sets in before noon. She can't hold a conversation when brain fog makes my thoughts feel like static. She's trained to help, yes, but she's not magic. She's a piece of my access plan. Not all of it.

Still, the assumption lingers. If I bring Lily, I shouldn't need anything else. I've even had people assume she was just there for emotional support. That I brought her because I was anxious, or lonely, or needed comfort. It's hard to explain that she's task-trained for medical alerts and mobility, not cuddles. She isn't a pet. She's my partner in navigating a world that wasn't built for me.

And it's not just students making those assumptions. Administrators, HR staff, even supervisors sometimes struggle to understand what a service dog really is. That misunderstanding often becomes policy.

I was once told I couldn't be within ten feet of pet therapy animals. A strange rule, considering both types of dogs are supposed to coexist in public spaces under federal law. I was also told that no one should ever interact with Lily-Rue. No petting, no speaking, no acknowledgment. At first, I understood the logic. She's working. She needs to focus.

But then I thought, what happens if I collapse? What if something happens to me, and no one feels they're allowed to approach her? What if the people I work with daily have been told to stay away, and in a moment of crisis, she hesitates to seek help from them? These rules, made in the name of structure and order, ignore the reality of our bond and the trust she builds with the people around me.

HR departments often add policies that sound official but have no basis in ADA law (Job Accommodation Network, n.d.). And when I push back, I'm not just advocating for myself. I'm trying to prevent the next person from being boxed in by a policy that was never written for us.

One moment that stands out to me was during a recent meeting. A staff member turned to me and asked, "Does Lily-Rue really need to be here for this?" The tone said more than the words. It wasn't curiosity. It was irritation, like our presence was a nuisance. I stayed calm. I asked politely, "Are you allergic to dogs or afraid of them?" They said no. They just thought service dogs were a distraction.

I tried to educate without becoming emotional, which is harder than people realize. It's hard to keep your voice steady when you're being asked, once again, to justify the existence of your lifeline. But sometimes, no matter how gently you speak, people don't want to understand.

This interaction wasn't the first of its kind, and I know it won't be the last. It's not just about one person's discomfort. It's about a broader failure to create space for disabled people to show up fully, with whatever tools they need to function safely and successfully.

To help foster understanding, here's a simple guide I wish more people would read before making assumptions as well as what not to ask (see Table 2).

Basic etiquette guide for interacting with people who use service dogs

1. Don't distract the dog—No petting, talking, whistling, or making eye contact. They're working.

2. Speak to the handler, not the dog—Treat the handler with the same respect you would anyone else.

3. Do not assume the dog is for emotional support—Service dogs are trained for specific medical tasks.

4. Don't ask intrusive questions—You don't need to know someone's diagnosis to treat them with dignity.

5. Trust the handler knows what they need—If they brought the dog, there's a reason.

6. If unsure, ask respectfully—But be ready to accept the answer and move on.

Disclosure becomes a constant calculation. What will they think? Will this change how they see me? What if I say too much, or not enough? What if I'm met with silence? Or worse, with doubt?

There's a strange grief that comes with disclosure. It's not just about the condition itself. It's about the way people look at you differently afterward. The shift in tone. The narrowed expectations. The subtle but unmistakable sense that your credibility has a new ceiling.

Because if we're serious about equity, we must stop asking disabled people to do all the explaining. And start asking systems to do better.

What support could look like instead

If we are serious about building more inclusive academic spaces, then we need to reconsider how we respond when someone shares that they are disabled, chronically ill, or navigating mental health challenges. Disclosure should not be a test of vulnerability or a prerequisite for respect. It should be met with care, curiosity, and a commitment to do better.

Too often, the reaction to disclosure is silence, awkward deflection, or worse unearned skepticism. But it doesn't have to be that way. Support doesn't require perfection. It requires presence. It requires the courage to move beyond defensiveness and into relationship.

If you don't know what to say when someone shares their diagnosis or access needs, here's a place to start:

- "Thank you for sharing this with me."
- "I appreciate that you trusted me with this information."
- "What strategies or accommodations help you most?"
- "Would you feel comfortable telling me more about your experiences?"
- "Is there anything I can do to support you better?"
- "Do you have any recommendations for where I can learn more about this?"

Table 2. What not to ask or assume about disabled people

What Not to Do	Why It's Harmful
Ask for someone's specific diagnosis	Medical information is private and not required for respectful interaction
Insist on "proof" of disability	Disability can be nonapparent and does not require validation from others
Treat accommodations as "special treatment"	Accommodations ensure equal access, not advantage
Assume a person "doesn't look disabled"	Disability comes in many forms, and appearances are not an indicator
Question the legitimacy of a service dog	If the dog is task-trained and well-behaved, it meets the legal definition
Compare one person's disability experience to another	Every disability journey is unique, and comparisons minimize lived experience

These words don't fix everything. But they open a door. They say: I see you. I'm listening. I want to do better.

It should never be the responsibility of the disabled person to earn understanding through disclosure. It should be the responsibility of the institution and its people to cultivate environments where understanding doesn't require disclosure in the first place.

We cannot build truly inclusive campuses if our policies demand vulnerability, but our people respond with indifference.

Support looks like learning. It looks like unlearning. And some-times, it looks like a quiet moment of acknowledgment—a sim-ple thank you that says, "You don't owe me an explanation. But I'm here if you want to share."

6
The service dog as disruption

Service dogs are trained to blend in, to move with calm precision, and to be unobtrusive and focused (Animal Behavior College, n.d.). And yet, no matter how well-trained Lily-Rue is, her presence in academic spaces rarely goes unnoticed. That's not a reflection of her. It's a reflection of the spaces she moves through.

This chapter explores how service dogs, while essential to their handlers, often challenge the unspoken rules of what professional, academic, and public spaces are "supposed" to look like. Their presence interrupts assumptions about productivity, appearance, and even authority.

I've seen it happen in classrooms, where instructors pause their lectures to address Lily before even acknowledging me. In HR offices, where people quietly shift their body language when we enter. In conference ballrooms, where conversations about inclusion are quickly followed by sideways glances at the dog at my feet. Even in restrooms—spaces that should be mundane—I've had people stop mid-step to ask if she's really allowed to be there, looking around nervously like we've broken an unspoken rule.

The disruption isn't always loud. Sometimes, it's subtle. A hesitancy. A lingering stare. An adjustment in tone. But it's there.

And with every entrance we make, there's a moment where space itself seems to pause, as if recalibrating for something unexpected. Not because Lily-Rue is doing anything wrong, but because her very presence calls attention to needs, realities, and rights that some would rather ignore.

In many professional and academic environments, there's an unspoken standard of who belongs and what belonging looks like. Service dogs, by their very nature, signal that someone in the room has needs that don't fit within those standards. Their presence demands a pause. A reconsideration. And that can make people uncomfortable.

But discomfort doesn't mean harm. Disruption isn't always negative. In fact, it can be the very thing that pushes a space toward growth.

Many times, I am blocked from access simply because people do not understand that federal law overrides institutional policies. I've had building staff stop me at the door and say, "No pets allowed," while pointing to signs clearly not meant for service animals. I've had event organizers ask me to wait outside while they double-check with someone higher up. Not because Lily-Rue was behaving inappropriately, but because they didn't understand she had a legal right to be there.

One moment that still lingers for me happened when I was working in career services as a career counselor. It was during a large, high-energy career fair, the kind with booths lined wall to wall and a constant hum of introductions and elevator pitches.

As I made my rounds, several employers commented on how "lucky" I was to be able to bring my dog to work with me. One smiled and asked, "So when does she have to go back to the organization?" assuming she was a dog-in-training. Another, in a tone laced with certainty, told me she couldn't possibly be a real service dog because I wasn't blind.

Their words were casual, thrown in between handshakes and business cards. But inside, I felt exposed. Reduced. Like my entire experience as a disabled professional was being publicly questioned and dismissed in a matter of seconds.

There's also the constant stream of people who reach for Lily-Rue without asking. Sometimes I stop them with a quick "She's working, please don't pet her." And sometimes, they get annoyed. One person looked offended and snapped, "Well why have a therapy dog if people can't pet her?" I had to pause, take a breath, and explain again: She's not a therapy dog. She's my medical equipment. My partner. She's not here for comfort. She's here to keep me safe.

These conversations are awkward. They're exhausting. And they're often very public. There is no privacy when you're forced to educate people everywhere you go. You can't schedule when these moments happen. You're just trying to attend a conference, use the restroom, or get through a workday and suddenly you're thrust into a teaching role you never volunteered for.

This chapter shares stories, mine and others 'of moments when service dogs disrupted the usual flow of higher education. A colleague whispering in a hallway that I was "lucky" to bring my dog to work, as if it were a perk. A restroom conversation turned awkward when someone mistook her for a pet I snuck in.

These are not isolated incidents. They are daily reminders that while service dogs support our access, they also expose how narrow our definitions of professionalism and presence can be.

To live and work with a service dog in higher education is to constantly ask: What does access really mean here? And who gets to define it?

It means facing disruptions with grace, but also with a willingness to hold space for truth. Because every time Lily-Rue walks beside me into a classroom, a meeting, or a conference, she is not just supporting me. She is challenging a system to stretch. To rethink. To include.

And sometimes, that disruption is exactly what the space needs.

Quick guide: Myths vs. facts about service dogs in higher education

To deepen understanding and spark meaningful dialogue, here's a more visually engaging breakdown of common misconceptions versus facts. Table 3 is intended as both a learning tool and a reminder that inclusive spaces require curiosity, not assumptions.

Table 3. Common myths and facts about service dogs

Myth	Fact
Service dogs are only for people who are blind.	Service dogs assist people with a variety of disabilities, including mobility, psychiatric, cardiac, and neurological conditions.
If a person doesn't "look disabled," the dog isn't necessary.	Many disabilities are nonapparent. You cannot determine someone need based on appearance.
You can't bring a dog into labs, restrooms, or dining halls.	Under the ADA, service dogs are allowed in all public areas unless their presence fundamentally alters the nature of the service provided.
If you're not actively using the dog at that moment, it isn't working.	Service dogs are always working when in public, even if they appear to be resting. They are monitoring, alerting, and ready to respond.
If a service dog is on campus, it must be in training.	Fully trained service dogs can accompany their handler throughout campus life. Not all handlers are trainers.
It's okay to ask personal medical questions to verify a dog's legitimacy.	It is illegal to ask about someone's diagnosis. Staff may only ask: (1) Is the dog a service animal? (2) What task is it trained to perform?

7
The duality of access: Human resources and student accessibility

When I first asked for accommodations at work, I wasn't looking for special treatment. I was asking for what should have been a given, the basic support guaranteed under the Americans with Disabilities Act. Instead, I found myself trapped in a maze of doubt, scrutiny, and resistance so subtle it felt like gaslighting.

The truth is, unless your disability is visible, something obvious to the naked eye, ADA protections often feel like a distant promise, not a lived reality. You become a suspect in your own life. Your pain, your exhaustion, your need for flexibility is questioned at every turn. You're expected to prove yourself over and over, like your body's betrayals aren't enough proof.

I remember the email from HR denying my request for a flexible work schedule. They pointed to the fact that I was teaching two overload courses and taking doctoral classes. The message was clear: because I was "doing so much," I couldn't possibly need accommodations. My success somehow invalidated my suffering. It was as if my ambition was held hostage to disbelief.

The process didn't stop there. Every step felt like wading through quicksand. I was asked to submit endless documentation, to explain myself in meetings that felt more like interrogations. My every move was monitored, every request dissected. I was no longer a professional; I was a problem to be managed.

Then there was Lily-Rue, my service dog and lifeline. She's the reason I can get through days that would otherwise break me. But even she wasn't safe from the institutional resistance. I got an email telling me to avoid a building during hours when therapy dogs were there. No offer to coordinate, no check-in about how this might impact my safety or dignity, just a cold directive to disappear. Therapy animals were celebrated; my service dog was expected to disappear quietly.

And when janitorial staff said they were uncomfortable cleaning my office with Lily around, I wasn't met with support or education. Instead, I was handed a vacuum and expected to clean my own workspace. It was humiliating. It said loud and clear that my needs were a burden.

This wasn't just policy failing; it was deeply personal. Each denial, each dismissive comment, chipped away at my dignity. I started to dread checking my inbox, bracing for the next demand to justify my disability, to prove I wasn't exploiting the system. I felt surveilled rather than supported, my efforts twisted into contradictions.

The toll was more than emotional; it became physical. My chronic pain worsened, my anxiety spiraled, and fatigue became debilitating. I cried in my car between meetings. I stopped eating regularly. Eventually, I needed medication to manage the anxiety consuming me. There were days so dark I questioned if I was broken, not by my illness, but by a system that weaponized it against me. I was not just unsupported; I was unwell. That unwellness was institutional.

Yet here I am. Not because the system made it easy, but because I refused to be silenced. My resilience isn't about bouncing back; it's about crawling forward when everything inside me wanted to stop. It's about naming the harm, resisting erasure, and healing on my own terms.

Rebuilding took tiny, stubborn acts of self-preservation: setting boundaries, seeking therapy, finding community, and allowing myself to be human in spaces that demanded otherwise. I learned that asking for help is strength, that rest is survival, and that advocacy from lived experience is a form of leadership.

I found mentors who saw me, students who reminded me why I fight, colleagues who helped me breathe again. Most importantly, I gave myself permission to take up space, not apologizing for my needs but owning my right to exist fully.

Healing is slow and messy. But every time I speak up, every time I write this story, I reclaim a piece of myself lost to doubt and dismissal. My healing is personal, political, ongoing.

Across campus, in a different office, my experience couldn't have been more different. Student Accessibility Services met me with care and respect from day one. I wasn't forced to relitigate my diagnosis or made to feel like a disruption. They coordinated accommodations openly, asked what else I needed, and never doubted my right to access. They treated Lily-Rue not as a problem but as a given.

That contrast, the cold suspicion of HR versus the warmth of Student Accessibility, exposed a painful truth: institutions can house both exclusion and inclusion. But when disability support is just a box to check, disabled professionals lose. When it's an opportunity to lead with equity, we gain.

This isn't just my story. It's the story of many disabled professionals, especially women of color, navigating a system that questions their worth before they even speak. Our bodies are labeled liabilities, our ambitions seen as contradictions. We're told to be competent enough to lead but silent enough not to disrupt. Too disabled for recognition, not disabled enough for support.

And yet, in the face of all this, I keep moving forward because I must, because the fight for access is a fight for dignity, for belonging, for justice. And because I refuse to make myself smaller to fit a world that wasn't made for me.

But my fight is not only for myself. It's for those who will come after me, those who may not have the resilience, the voice, or the stamina to push back against denial and say no to "no." I want to be the person who clears the path, who opens the door wider, so that others don't have to fight the same exhausting battles just to exist. I want to advocate for those whose strength is taxed before they even get started and whose voices are too often drowned out. Because none of us should have to make ourselves small to belong.

A human-centered approach: How HR should proceed

If HR departments truly want to support disabled professionals, they must begin by unlearning their assumptions. Disability isn't always visible, and it isn't linear (Bezyak et al., 2024) And it isn't something to be managed away with a policy manual.

Below are ten actionable steps for building an HR culture that genuinely supports dynamic disabilities and service dog handlers:

1. **Believe people the first time**

    Start from a place of trust. When an employee discloses a need, assume truth not exaggeration.

2. **Align with ADA, not against it**

    Avoid adding additional requirements or documentation that exceed federal guidelines. Policies should facilitate access, not block it.

3. **Normalize remote and flexible Work**

    Understand that flexibility is often the difference between burnout and sustainability. Remote work is a right, not a luxury.

4. **Train everyone on service animal law**

    From front desk staff to event planners, ensure everyone knows the difference between service dogs and therapy animals and who has legal access.

5. **Respond with collaboration, not correction**

    If there's confusion about how an accommodation fits within job duties, schedule a meeting with the employee not an interrogation.

6.   Empower internal advocates

Designate trained accessibility liaisons within HR who can offer empathetic, knowledgeable guidance on navigating the accommodation process.

7.   Center disability in institutional equity work

Include disabled voices in all DEI programming. Accessibility should not be a footnote it should be embedded throughout the institution.

8.   Reject productivity as proof of health

Don't use someone's output as a reason to deny their pain. High performance often comes at high personal cost.

9.   Create clear policies for handling conflicts

When janitorial staff, coworkers, or supervisors resist disability accommodations, there should be established, inclusive procedures not workarounds that penalize the disabled employee.

10.   Always, lead with care

Disability support must be guided by dignity. Policies matter, but people matter more.

Until we adopt these practices not just in writing but in behavior, institutions will continue to push out the very professionals they claim to support. The choice to stay in higher education shouldn't have to come at the cost of well-being. And no one should have to prove their pain to earn their place.

8
Learning while leading

There's a certain irony to being both a student and a staff member in higher education—especially when you're disabled. You're positioned to learn from systems while simultaneously trying to survive them. You are expected to lead with professionalism while navigating environments that often do not see or accommodate your full humanity.

For me, pursuing an Ed.D. wasn't just about earning another degree. It was about making sense of the very systems I was trying to change. Every class discussion on leadership theory, every assignment on organizational behavior, every case study about inclusive policy—it all felt deeply personal. Because I wasn't just writing about equity. I was living the absence of it.

My dual identity meant I was always walking a line. As a staff member, I was expected to uphold the institution's values. As a student with a disability, I often bore witness to the many ways those values were not applied consistently or compassionately. I could recite ADA policy, cite best practices, and still find myself explaining, once again, why my service dog should be allowed in a space. Why sitting down during a presentation wasn't a sign of weakness. Why remote work was not a request for convenience, but a lifeline during medical flares.

I lived in the in—between. Between policy and practice. And that gap—the space between what's written and what's lived—is where so much harm happens. Policies are meant to offer protection, structure, clarity. But without understanding, implementation, and accountability, policies become little more than performative promises. On paper, I was protected. I had the right to accommodations. The right to access. The right to bring my service dog into spaces I needed to be in. But in practice, I was questioned, redirected, and at times, outright excluded.

Between policy and practice is where I was told to step aside for pet therapy dogs. Where I was handed a vacuum instead of being offered support. Where I had to explain the legitimacy of my dog to colleagues who had read the policy but didn't understand it. It's the space where institutions say all the right things in public but quietly ask you to shrink yourself in private.

That in-between space is where good intentions and reality don't always meet. It's where HR staff, some well-meaning and some openly ableist, cling to outdated procedures. It's where inclusion committees forget to make events accessible, even while claiming to value diversity. Faculty know the ADA exists, but many feel unprepared to apply it without disrupting their syllabus. And in all that, disabled professionals like me end up doing the invisible work: educating, reminding, accommodating, and carrying everyone else's discomfort, just to stay afloat ourselves.

Living between policy and practice is not just exhausting—it's a full—time job. One we didn't apply for. One we do out of necessity, not choice.

The hardest part wasn't always the policies. It was the people. The colleagues who looked away when I walked into a meeting with Lily-Rue. The supervisors who called my commitment into question because I was asking for what I needed to do my job. The casual tone of disbelief in emails that asked, in so many words, "Are you sure you're disabled enough?"

What made it harder was that I knew how to navigate the system. I knew what forms to file, what language to use, how to present my case with professionalism. And still, it often wasn't enough. I felt like I had to become the teachable moment in every room. My body, my dog, my requests—all became a lesson in inclusion for others. Whether I consented or not.

Being a disabled student while working full time in higher education is not just exhausting. It is revealing. It exposes the fragility of performative inclusion. It shows where support ends, and tolerance begins. And it reminds you, again, that until institutions truly see and include disability as part of leadership, we will remain on the margins.

But the truth is, leadership while disabled especially while also learning is exhausting. It is the kind of fatigue that settles in your bones, the kind that no weekend off or wellness email can resolve. It's not just the physical toll of managing a dynamic disability while meeting deadlines. It's the emotional weight of having to explain, defend, and educate constantly often with a smile that masks the strain. There is fatigue in the constant double-checking of how you're perceived, in fearing that asking for what you need will cost you credibility. It's tiring to carry the weight of being someone's learning moment, while also carrying the weight of your own unmet needs.

But I've also learned something powerful: There is a different kind of leadership that emerges from this experience. It's not polished. It's not always confident. But it is deeply rooted in truth. It's the kind of leadership that knows how to hold space. That knows when to speak and when to listen. That recognizes the weight of being first, or only, or one of few.

But before I came to that truth, I lived many moments that tested it. I remember one graduate seminar where I arrived late—not because I was unprepared, but because I had to navigate a building with no elevator access to the classroom. When I arrived, flustered and out of breath, the professor barely glanced up. No one paused to ask if I was okay. I sat quietly, aware that my dog drew more attention than my contributions ever would. That night, we discussed leadership traits, and the irony was not lost on me: adaptability, resilience, empathy—traits that I lived everyday were listed on the screen as bullet points, while I sat invisible in plain sight.

There was another moment—maybe more painful because it was quieter—when a student I was mentoring asked for guidance on managing a difficult conversation with a professor about accommodations. I gave her my full attention, validating her feelings, offering strategies, walking her through her options. She left with her head held high. I sat alone afterward and thought, *who is helping me navigate mine?*

Even routine tasks carried extra weight. Walking into a room with Lily-Rue meant scanning every face for that subtle change— curiosity, discomfort, judgment. "She's a real service dog?" some- one once whispered behind me. I smiled politely, though my body stiffened. *How many times do I have to explain this?* Every interaction like that pulled me out of the moment and into defense mode. And that mode became my default.

In a course on leadership ethics, we studied the importance of modeling values. I couldn't help but wonder—what values are modeled when disabled staff are taught to hide?

I've come to believe that true leadership—especially for those of us with disabilities is not about perfection. It's about visibil- ity. It's about showing up fully, even when it's uncomfortable for others. It's about bringing the truth into spaces that have long sanitized it.

What it means to lead with disability

To lead with disability is to lead with flexibility, because we have had to pivot when others pushed back. It's to lead with patience, because change moves slowly, especially for us. It's to lead with strategy, because we've learned how to navigate resistance with language, law, and grace. It's to lead with heart, because no one else is holding ours with care.

It's not about heroism. It's about honesty. It's about saying, "I need rest" without guilt. It's about saying, "I belong here" without apol- ogy. It's about letting others see us not just as advocates, but as architects of the very systems we were told we could never access.

This chapter is not just a reflection. It's a reclamation. Of space. Of voice. Of the right to lead while learning. To teach while accommodating. To build while grieving.

Because disability is not a deficit in leadership. It is a lens—a powerful one. And those of us navigating higher education from both sides of the desk have something urgent to say—not just about what we've survived, but about what we are here to change.

If institutions truly want to foster equitable leadership, they must start listening to the people who have led through resistance. We are not the exception. We are the evidence of what systems fail to see. It's time to stop asking disabled professionals to lead quietly. It's time to make space for leadership that includes, reflects, and honors all of us.

9
Policy vs. practice

Higher education institutions proudly claim to champion inclusivity, equity, and equality. These words are plastered across mission statements, diversity statements, and strategic plans. Campuses host workshops, launch initiatives, and celebrate marginalized identities during designated months. At a glance, it seems like progress is being made, that these institutions are committed to creating spaces where everyone, regardless of background or ability, can thrive.

But the reality often tells a different story. Beneath these polished declarations lies a gap between rhetoric and reality—a gap that disabled students and employees know all too well. The systems and structures in place frequently fail to live up to these lofty ideals. What is touted as inclusion can sometimes feel more like tokenism, and what is called equity too often looks like standardization or rigid uniformity.

Policies are often crafted with good intentions, yet their implementation can betray those very intentions. For example, universities may boast about accessible campuses but continue to design buildings and classrooms that exclude people with mobility challenges or sensory sensitivities. They may proclaim support for disabled students but require convoluted documentation processes that create barriers rather than pathways.

Faculty might receive training on equity, but when confronted with real accommodation requests, they default to suspicion or misconceived fairness arguments that ignore individual needs.

Equity and equality are frequently conflated, creating confusion and frustration. Equality implies treating everyone the same, while equity means recognizing and addressing individual differences to ensure fair outcomes (Braveman & Gruskin, 2003). Too often, institutions settle for equality applying one-size-fits-all policies that ignore the nuanced realities of disability. This approach can inadvertently reinforce exclusion by demanding conformity to norms that were never designed with diversity in mind.

Furthermore, the culture within many academic institutions can be unforgiving to those who don't fit the mold (Kerschbaum et al., 2017). Disabled professionals and students may be admired for their persistence, but that admiration sometimes comes with a caveat: they must prove their worth repeatedly and never ask for too much. The pressure to "pass" as able-bodied, to mask struggles, or to minimize accommodations is immense.

In short, the promises of inclusivity and equity often ring hollow when the lived experience of disabled individuals is taken into account. This disconnect is not just frustrating; it's harmful. It sends the message that disability is an inconvenience, that accommodations are favors rather than rights, and that the institution's image matters more than genuine belonging.

To truly practice what it preaches, higher education must confront this gap head-on. It requires more than policies and statements; it demands a fundamental shift in mindset and culture. It means listening to disabled voices, dismantling ableist norms, and embedding accessibility into every aspect of campus life not as an afterthought but as a core value.

Only then can the ideals of inclusivity, equity, and equality become realities, not just slogans.

The policies aren't always the problem. The way they're interpreted is.

From policy to practice: Where institutions go wrong

1. **Assuming compliance equals inclusion**

   Meeting the bare minimum of the law does not ensure a student or staff member feels safe, respected, or valued.

2. **Creating extra requirements**

   Requiring documentation, training credentials, or "permission" for access often exceeds ADA and Section 504 requirements.

3. **Siloing disability services**

   When accessibility offices are left out of curriculum planning, hiring practices, or DEI initiatives, inclusion becomes optional instead of integrated.

4. **Relying on punitive language**

   Policies written to anticipate misuse or disruption rather than collaboration send the message that disabled people are a risk to manage.

5. **Failing to consult disabled voices**

   Disabled students and employees are the experts in their own access. Policies developed without their input often miss the mark entirely.

Bridging the gap: Recommendations for moving forward

- **Train everyone, not just disability staff**

  Faculty, supervisors, custodial staff, advisors everybody should understand the basics of ADA, universal design, and how to respond when someone discloses a need (Job Accommodation Network, n.d.).

- **Audit existing policies with a human lens**

  Review your accommodation processes for barriers. Is the tone punitive? Are the forms accessible? Does it feel like a support system or a defense mechanism?

- **Center disabled voices in co-designed policymaking**

  Form advisory boards that include disabled faculty, staff, and students. Pay them for their time and treat their insights as professional expertise.

- **Make transparency a standard, not a request**

  Ensure students and staff know their rights, and where to go for support. Hide nothing behind fine print or backchannel approval processes.

- **Remember the spirit of the law**

  Compliance is not the ceiling. It is the floor. If policies aren't fostering trust, dignity, and inclusion they are failing, even if they are legal.

Bridging the gap between policy and practice is not just an administrative challenge. It is a cultural one. And until institutions treat disability inclusion as a shared responsibility not a legal checkbox, we will continue to fall short of the equity we claim to value.

10
Building back better: Beyond accommodation

When I first entered higher education as a staff member and doctoral student with a disability, I believed that existing policies, ADA, Section 504, institutional procedures would be enough. That access would follow policy, and belonging would follow access. But it didn't take long to realize that accommodations are often where the conversation starts and stops.

Accommodation is not the goal. It's the floor. And too often, it becomes the ceiling.

Over the years, I've worked with academic departments and campus leadership across diverse disciplines from medicine to engineering, education to mathematics. And regardless of the field, one truth remains: accessibility is treated as a reactive measure rather than a built-in value. The social model of disability helps us understand why.

The social model tells us that disability is not rooted in the individual body, but in the environment that excludes it (Shakespeare, 2013). Barriers are not just ramps or stairs they're assumptions, policies, cultural habits, and institutional silos. When a student with a chronic illness is penalized for absences in a course without flexible attendance policies, it's not their body that is the barrier. It's the system.

To build back better, higher education must move beyond individualized accommodation and toward a fully integrated access culture.

Designing for belonging: From silo to system

I remember sitting in a room with leaders from five different colleges: Education, Engineering, Medicine, Science & Math, and the Veterinary School. Each had their own approach to accessibility. Some hadn't thought much about it. Others wanted to help but weren't sure how.

One person asked, "Do we really need to think about disability in all these different spaces? Can't that just live with the accessibility office?"

I looked around and said, "If inclusion only lives in one office, what happens when the door closes?"

Inclusion cannot be outsourced. It must live everywhere. It must live in the policies we co-create the labs we build, the syllabi we hand out, and the assumptions we challenge.

What real commitment looks like

Every college whether it's working with cadavers or coding should have:

- An accessibility liaison who works with students, staff, and faculty.
- Regular audits of fieldwork, internships, and classroom design.

- Training that goes beyond ADA checklists and centers lived experience.

In the College of Medicine, this might mean redesigning simulation labs so a service dog can be present without compromising hygiene. In the College of Engineering, it might mean rethinking project timelines for students with fluctuating conditions. In the College of Education, it means preparing future teachers to use Universal Design for Learning (UDL) as the foundation, not the supplement. Universal Design for Learning (UDL) is based on the idea that all students, not just the "standard" one, should be able to use classrooms and learning resources effectively. As an alternative to forcing all students to conform to a predetermined curriculum, UDL encourages teachers to create flexible classes that provide all students enough opportunities to participate, learn, and demonstrate what they've learned. Building a ramp instead of just stairs is the analogy I'm using. Everyone can reach their destination regardless of their walking style. Accessibility, friendliness, and flexibility in learning have always been at the heart of UDL (CAST, 2018).

These aren't extras. These are expectations for institutions that claim equity as a core value.

Words matter: Syllabi and web presence

In my consulting, I've worked with colleagues and students to rewrite accessibility language in syllabi and on their websites. Too often, it's reduced to a compliance paragraph at the bottom of the page.

What if, instead, every syllabus began with:

> *"This course embraces access as a shared responsibility. Disability is welcome here. Accommodations are not special treatment they are tools for equity. If you have access needs, let's talk about how this space can work better for you."*

Or every college landing page said:

> *"We believe access belongs at the center. Our college partners with accessibility services, the disability student union, and disabled faculty and staff to build a culture where inclusion is proactive not an afterthought."*

This is more than messaging. It's mindset.

Onboarding and orientation: Setting the tone

The first messages students and employees receive matter. Orientation is the perfect opportunity to shape expectations around disability not as liability, but as leadership.

Orientation should include:

- A segment on disability justice and institutional values
- A guide to how and where to access accommodations
- A training video on service dogs, with clear instructions for respectful interaction (Animal Behavior College, n.d.).
- Testimonies from disabled students and employees who have shaped the campus

When we normalize disability from the start, we don't need to keep re-explaining ourselves later.

The role of disability justice

The social model helps us diagnose the problem, but disability justice shows us the way forward. It asks:

- Who gets left behind when access is only reactive?
- Whose stories are never invited into the room?
- What does real inclusion look like when we design with not for disabled people?

Disability justice centers the most impacted. It reminds us that accessibility is not just about ramps and captions. It's about relationships, interdependence, and the belief that all bodies belong.

> We must not only accommodate. We must redesign.
> We must not only consult. We must co-create.
> We must not only include. We must shift the culture.

A truly inclusive university is one where service dogs are as common as backpacks, where syllabi include access language alongside learning outcomes, and where disability is not something to "work around "but something that reshapes the very structure of how we work together.

That is what it means to build back better.

Not just access. Not just equity. A culture where no one must ask if they belong because they already do.

11
Lily-Rue's legacy: A story of becoming

I didn't always think I was "disabled enough" to need a service dog. If I'm being honest, I spent a long time convincing myself I could just tough it out just try harder, just get by, just not need so much. But bodies have a way of cutting through denial, and eventually, the bad days started piling up. Too many times, I found myself stuck on the couch, at the door, in the damn cereal aisle wishing someone or something could help me get through.

The idea of a service dog started as a whisper. I tried to push it away. We already had four dogs at home, for God's sake. My mom's patience for animal chaos was already stretched to the limit. But the more I tried to "just manage," the clearer it became: my world was shrinking, and I was running out of ways to hide it.

It took weeks, maybe months, to work up the nerve to even bring it up. I practiced the conversation in my head, mapped out all my reasons, braced for the "don't we have enough animals?" talk. One night, in the kitchen, I just blurted it out: "I think I need a service dog." My mom gave me this looks the kind only moms can pull off equal parts concern, skepticism, and that tired love of someone who's already juggling too much.

And of course, reality hit hard. I couldn't afford a fully trained service dog. Not even close. I started googling, just to torture myself, and saw the numbers: $15,000, $30,000, $45,000. There was no way. Even if I sold everything I owned, I wouldn't get close. So, I started digging into the world of self-training. Not everyone recommends it. Honestly, the odds aren't great. You can do everything right and still end up with a dog who just isn't cut out for the job wrong temperament, too anxious, too stubborn, too much of a goofball. Service work is hard. Not every dog is meant for it.

But I couldn't shake the feeling that this was my best shot. I told my mom, "I know it sounds crazy, but what if I got a puppy? I could work with a local trainer do the hard stuff myself, learn as I go." It sounded shaky, even to me. She sighed, looked at our existing herd, and finally said, "If you really think this is what you need, we'll figure it out."

When we went to see the litter, I was terrified I'd pick wrong. What if I bonded with the wrong puppy? What if none of them had the right temperament? What if I spent months training, pouring my hope into this little animal, and she just… couldn't do it? The breeder let me sit on the floor with the puppies. Most of them bounced around, wild and squirmy, but one little girl just sat in my lap, calm and curious, looking up like she was already waiting for instructions. That was Lily-Rue.

Bringing her home was equal parts hope and dread. The odds were not in my favor. I read everything I could about service dog training, made charts, set alarms, scheduled sessions with a local trainer who didn't sugarcoat anything: "Most dogs wash out. Don't get attached to the idea it has to work." I nodded, but inside, I was already attached.

Training was nothing like the YouTube videos. There were days Lily seemed to get it, and days she was more interested in chasing her tail than learning a new task. I'd wonder if I was messing everything up. Was I being too hard? Not hard enough? Was I asking too much of her, too much of myself? Sometimes I'd sit on the floor next to her crate, head in my hands, and just wish I knew what the hell I was doing.

But there were moments small, quiet ones that kept me going. The first time she nudged me before I could even feel the start of a flare. The way she watched me, alert and steady, when I was having a rough morning. The way she'd come and sit by my side, no matter how many other dogs were vying for attention.

It wasn't easy. We failed at things. We had to start over. There was always that fear in the back of my mind: What if she can't do this? What if I can't do this? But we kept going, stubborn in our own ways.

Now, when people see us together, they don't know the whole story. They don't see the late nights, the second-guessing, the mess of it all. They see a calm, focused dog and a handler who, finally, doesn't look like they're barely holding it together. I still get the questions "Are you training her for someone else?" "What's wrong with you? "And I still have days where I want to shrink away. But Lily doesn't care. She just shows up, every time, ready to work.

She's gotten me through more than I can count bad days, hard conversations, moments I would have skipped if I could have. She's made it possible for me to show up, to be seen, to need what I need without apology.

I used to think needing less made you stronger. Now I know: letting yourself need, and trusting someone or some dog enough to meet you there? That's strength. That's survival.

She's, my proof.

I owe a lot to my trainer at Full-Service Canine. Honestly, I don't think I'd be here, writing this, or even walking through the world the way I do, if I hadn't had that support. From the very beginning, they were honest about the challenges. No sugarcoating. They told me, straight up, how tough it is to self-train a service dog the odds, the heartbreak if things don't pan out, the amount of patience it takes. But they also looked at me like I was capable, even on days when I was sure I wasn't.

There were mornings when Lily-Rue was more interested in chewing socks than learning anything useful, afternoons when I felt like I was flunking out of some invisible test. My trainer never made me feel like I was failing. If Lily-Rue had an off day, or I did, my trainer reminded me, "Progress isn't linear. Some days are just about showing up." They celebrated the tiny wins with me—a successful alert, a calm sit in a crowded place, Lily-Rue ignoring an entire chicken nugget on the sidewalk. I learned that the little moments matter.

It wasn't just about the dog, it was about me, too. There were so many times I doubted myself as a handler. I worried I was too inconsistent or too anxious, or that I'd mess Lily up somehow.

My trainer saw all that, and instead of judging, they would break things down, make it manageable, give me permission to laugh at the chaos. When I needed tough love, they delivered it. When I needed reassurance, they knew how to give that too.

Thanks to that support, I'm not just someone with a service dog, I'm a service dog handler. There's a difference. I've learned to read Lily-Rue's body language, to anticipate her needs, to trust her judgment as much as my own. Training together wasn't about creating the "perfect" dog. It was about building a partnership that worked for us. And while Lily-Rue might not be perfect by anyone else's standards she has her quirks, her stubborn streaks, her moments of distraction she is perfect for me. She's the dog who needed me as much as I needed her.

People see us now, moving as a team, and they have no idea how much we both learned, how many times we almost gave up, or how much credit goes to the trainer who believed in both of us. I'm grateful every single day for that. Lily-Rue might not be perfect, but she is, without a doubt, exactly who I needed. And honestly, that's all that matters.

What Lily-Rue taught me about disability and leadership

If you'd asked me years ago what leadership looked like, I'd have described someone who always knew what to say, who could rally a team or step up in a crisis, who made hard things look easy. I thought leadership was all about performance projecting confidence, masking uncertainty, moving fast and never letting anyone see how tired you really were.

And then came Lily-Rue.

Lily is not a headline act. She's the steady presence beside me unfazed, attentive, never asking for more than I can give. On my worst days, when my body feels like it's made of glass or every step is a negotiation, she doesn't flinch or look away. She just sits, patient and calm, as if to say: I'm here, and that's enough. There's a power in her quiet consistency that has taught me more about real leadership than any book or seminar ever could.

What I didn't expect, when Lily-Rue entered my life, was that she would become a bridge. Suddenly, my presence on campus became an invitation not just for stares or passing curiosity, but for real conversations. It started with a trickle: a student hesitantly approaching me outside the library, eyes flicking between me and Lily, voice low. "I've seen you with your dog can I ask what she does?" Sometimes the questions came from students who'd never considered that service animals aren't just for people with visible disabilities. Other times, they came from students who, quietly, wanted to know if a service dog could help them too if they were "disabled enough," if there was a place for support in their own lives.

There were days when I'd find myself stopped three, four, five times walking across campus by students, staff, even visitors. They wanted to know: How does she help you? What's the difference between a service dog and an emotional support animal? Can service dogs go everywhere? What does the training look like? Sometimes these questions were practical. Sometimes they were laced with hope, or even relief, as if, by seeing Lily and me together, they'd found a kind of permission to wonder about their own access, their own needs.

These conversations never felt burdensome. If anything, they felt urgent like cracks of light in a system that so often tells us to hide what we need. Every time I paused to answer someone's questions, I could see the ripple effect: a little less stigma, a little more understanding. Sometimes, students would circle back weeks later with updates: "I talked to my counselor about accommodations," or "I told my roommate what I learned about service animals." More than once, someone has told me, "I never knew this was even possible for someone like me."

And it's not just on campus. When I visit new places for my job, Lily-Rue is my visible counterpart. People watch us walk in, sometimes with curiosity, sometimes with skepticism. But by the time I leave after the meeting, the event, or the workshop—folks always carry more knowledge out the door than they brought in. I've watched entire rooms shift from awkward silence to open dialogue just because someone finally asked, "What does your dog do for you?" Suddenly, the conversation isn't just about policy or compliance—it's about real lives, real barriers, and the possibilities that open up when we stop pretending everyone's needs are the same.

I've come to see these moments as small acts of advocacy, the kind that build change slowly, one honest conversation at a time. Lily-Rue is always the catalyst: she opens doors that would otherwise stay closed, softens people's defenses, makes it safe to ask what they're usually too embarrassed to voice. She gives me a way to model what it looks like to show up with your support visible, unapologetic, and essential.

Through it all, Lily has taught me that leadership isn't about commanding attention or being the loudest voice in the room. It's about showing up, consistently, with patience and presence. It's about making room for questions, holding space for uncertainty, and meeting people where they are even if that's a hallway, a busy office, or the edge of a crowded quad. She reminds me that sometimes the most powerful thing you can do is simply to be visible, to answer honestly, and to let others see that it's okay to need help.

Because of Lily-Rue, I've learned that leadership is about opening doors sometimes literally, sometimes in the quieter ways that change how people see themselves, and what they believe is possible.

The invisible work we carry

There are so many things people don't see: the hours spent finding accessible entrances, the careful calculations of where to sit in a classroom or conference, the preemptive emails explaining her presence, the conversations I've had to repeat, softly but firmly, to people who want to pet her, question her, or deny her.

By the time I sit at a meeting table, I've already scanned the room, clocked every exit, gauged the vibe. That's the cost of bringing a service dog into spaces where education doesn't begin until we walk in. Her presence has been the catalyst for hard conversations and the comfort I needed after them. She has helped me reimagine advocacy not as a loud performance, but as a steady walk beside someone who sees all of you and stays anyway.

As I think about the legacy of this work, I know that Lily-Rue will not always be here. That is a grief I am already holding quietly. But her impact will outlast her working years. Because of her, I've been brave enough to write this book. To speak up when it was uncomfortable. To trust that someone, somewhere, might read these pages and feel a little less alone.

Lily-Rue's legacy is not just about service. It's about presence. It's about changing the way we understand leadership, care, and community. And it's about honoring the truth that no access work, no justice warrior, has ever been done alone.

She is my heartbeat, my shadow, my reminder that even in the most inaccessible spaces, love and connection still make room.

And if she has taught me anything, it's this: we deserve that room.

We always have.

A closing note to readers

If you've made it this far, thank you. Thank you for sitting with these stories, these policies, and these moments of vulnerability and truth. Writing this book was never just a personal endeavor. It was a risk I took, fueled by hope and a deep love for every disabled person navigating institutions that were never designed with us in mind. This book is, in many ways, a love letter to you, a recognition of the courage it takes to show up in spaces that often feel unwelcoming, confusing, or even hostile.

I hope these chapters have given you something you can hold onto, something real and tangible. Whether that's validation that your experiences matter, language to articulate your needs and rights, or the courage to stand up and challenge practices that no longer serve you or your community. If you are a student trying to find your place, a staff member balancing work and health, a faculty member striving to teach inclusively, an administrator working to create better policies, or an advocate pushing for change, I hope this book reminds you that the work of access is not about perfection. It is about presence. It is about showing up for one another, listening more than defending, and being willing to reshape systems and cultures that have existed unchanged for far too long.

Access is not a checklist to be completed or a box to be ticked. It is a culture, a way of being that must be nurtured, practiced daily, protected fiercely, and passed forward to those who will continue this vital work into the future. This responsibility does not fall solely on the shoulders of those labeled disabled. It belongs to all of us, because everyone benefits from a world that is more just, more flexible, and more inclusive.

To the disabled reader, know this: you are not too much. You are not a burden or an inconvenience. You are living, breathing proof of what this world has yet to fully see or understand. You represent the imagination and courage needed to push society forward, to question norms, and to demand spaces where everyone can belong. Your presence challenges old assumptions and invites new ways of thinking about ability, value, and community. You deserve to occupy space fully, loudly if you wish, and without apology.

To the ally reading this, keep going. Keep learning, even when it's uncomfortable or when you feel unsure. Don't wait for the perfect words, the perfect moment, or the perfect understanding before you act. Begin where you are, with presence and intention. Ask thoughtful questions that open dialogue rather than shut it down. Know when to step back and make room for disabled voices, and when to step forward and use your privilege to advocate and support. Uplift disabled voices without expecting them to educate or explain on demand. Remember, allyship is not a destination or a label, it is a continuous practice, a commitment to growth and humility.

To every service dog handler reading this, you are deeply seen and honored. The work you do every day, the advocacy you engage in, the patience required to explain, the self-restraint you show when others misunderstand, and the persistence you embody is nothing short of revolutionary. Your dog is not a tool, nor a distraction, nor a pet for others' comfort. Your dog is your teammate, your lifeline, and your partner in navigating a world that often refuses to understand. You deserve spaces where both of you are welcomed fully and unconditionally, spaces where your presence is respected and your partnership honored.

If there is one truth, I hope you carry from this book, it is this: we are not asking for special treatment or favors. We are simply asking to be included in the world as it should be, whole, messy, complex, and profoundly human. We are asking for a society where difference is not erased or hidden but embraced and celebrated.

This work is far from finished, and in many ways, it always will be. But it is sacred. Each step forward, every barrier that falls, every voice raised in solidarity brings us closer to a future where disability is not something to accommodate away or erase, but something that is woven into the very fabric of our communities, enriching them in ways we have yet to fully imagine.

May we continue to build that future together, with courage, with compassion, and with hope.

Assignments and discussion starters

For future educators, advocates and changemakers

(Disability Studies & Teacher Education Edition)

1. **Reflect: What does belonging really look like in a classroom?**

    Think about a time when you (or someone close to you) didn't feel fully welcome in a classroom. What was said—or not said—that made the space feel unsafe or inaccessible? Now imagine yourself as an educator. What would you do differently? Inspired by *Invisible Leashes*, write a 3–5 page reflection exploring how teachers shape culture—sometimes through small choices that speak volumes. This is your chance to think about what kind of educator you want to be, and why inclusion can't be performative, it must be personal.

2. **Policies with people in mind**

    Policies are everywhere in education—but are they written with real students in mind? Choose a disability-related policy from your school, university, or state (e.g., service dog access, 504 plans, flexible attendance). Read it like someone who's lived the story in *Invisible Leashes*. What's missing? Whose voice isn't heard? Then rewrite a section (even just a paragraph) to feel more human—less red tape, more real-life care. Add a short note explaining why your changes matter.

3. **Design a classroom that doesn't just "include"—it welcomes**

    Picture your future classroom. Now imagine a student with a dynamic disability or a service dog joining your class. How will you set the tone? What will you say when curious classmates ask questions? Create a short guide—for yourself or fellow teachers—on how to build a culture of respect, boundaries, and warmth. Use your voice. Make it kind. Make it useful. Imagine how one student might breathe easier because you thought ahead.

4. **Lead with curiosity, not perfection**

    Choose a section from *Invisible Leashes* that made you pause. What truth did it name? What made you feel uncomfortable—or seen? Use it to design a 30-minute classroom conversation. You don't need to be an expert; just be willing to ask the questions that matter: How does ableism show up in our schools? What does it really mean to "accommodate" someone? How do we sit with stories that challenge what we thought we knew? Write up your plan with care—your classmates might learn more from your honesty than from any textbook.

5. **Who are you—and how will that shape the space you hold?**

    As future educators and advocates, your identities will walk into every classroom with you. Create a visual identity map—race, gender, disability, culture, class, religion, values—and write a 2–3 page reflection. Which parts of you feel celebrated? Which feel misunderstood? What might this mean for how you see your students, especially those who move through the world differently? This is less about having the answers, and more about starting the kind of self-awareness that makes room for *everyone*.

Books that stay with you: Recommended further reading

Disability visibility, edited by Alice Wong

This is more than a book—it's a gathering of voices. Raw, honest, and full of life, these essays by disabled writers will expand how you think about justice, survival, and what it means to be seen. Read it when you need to remember that your story matters, and so do the voices we don't hear enough.

Care work, by Leah Lakshmi Piepzna-Samarasinha

Part manifesto, part poetry, part survival guide, *Care work* reminds us that community care isn't a backup plan—it's the foundation. It holds space for messiness, interdependence, and the kind of radical tenderness that disabled people have been practicing all along.

Academic ableism, by Jay Dolmage

If you've ever wondered why higher education feels so inaccessible sometimes—this book names it. Sharp, clear, and unafraid, it calls out the ableist systems baked into classrooms, policies, and buildings. And it invites us to imagine something better. Something more human.

Being Heumann, by Judith Heumann

Judith's story is unforgettable. From being denied access to school to leading protests that shaped national law, her fight for disability rights is deeply personal and profoundly inspiring. It's a reminder that one person's voice can change everything.

Demystifying disability, by Emily Ladau

Think of this as the friendly guide you wish everyone had. Emily breaks down disability etiquette, language, and allyship in a way that's accessible, compassionate, and real. No judgment—just an open invitation to do better and be kinder.

References

Anderson, A. (n.d.). A woman's take on intersectionality through the lens of disability. Retrieved from https://alyciaanderson.com/a-womans-take-on-intersectionality-through-the-lens-of-disability/?srsltid=AfmBOoqLaI1ePIZb8TtAwDyChWnoWeZ1gFdtuTe1w9BSrllWHsjdD8me

Animal Behavior College. (n.d.). Service dog trainer curriculum. https://www.animalbehaviorcollege.com/service-dog-trainer/curriculum/

Bezyak, J., Versen, E., Chan, F., Lee, D., Wu, J. R., Iwanaga, K., Rumrill, P., Chen, X., & Ho, H. (2024). Needs of human resource professionals in implicit bias and disability inclusion training: A focus group study. *Journal of Vocational Rehabilitation*, 60(3), 311–319.

Braveman, P., & Gruskin, S. (2003). Defining equity in health. *Journal of Epidemiology & Community Health*, 57(4), 254–258. https://doi.org/10.1136/jech.57.4.254

CAST. (2018). Universal Design for Learning guidelines version 2.2. http://udlguidelines.cast.org

Job Accommodation Network. (n.d.). Educating the workforce about the ADA and accommodations. AskJAN. https://askjan.org/articles/Educating-the-Workforce-about-the-ADA-and-Accommodations.cfm

Kerschbaum, S. L., Eisenman, L. T., & Jones, J. M. (2017). Negotiating disability: Disclosure and higher education. University of Michigan Press.

Miserandino, C. (2003). The spoon theory. But You Don't Look Sick. http://www.butyoudontlooksick.com/articles/written-by-christine/the-spoon-theory/

Shakespeare, T. (2013). Disability rights and wrongs revisited (2nd ed.). Routledge.

Wadman, M. (2024, March 7). No dogs allowed: Service dogs still face barriers to labs and fieldwork. Science. https://www.science.org/content/article/no-dogs-allowed-service-dogs-still-face-barriers-labs-and-fieldwork

Index